Reprints of Economic Classics

ECONOMIC STUDIES

ECONOMIC STUDIES

BY

WALTER BAGEHOT

EDITED BY

RICHARD HOLT HUTTON

[1898]

AUGUSTUS M. KELLEY • PUBLISHERS
CLIFTON 1973

First Edition 1895
Fourth Impression 1898

(*London*: Longmans, Green and Company, *39 Paternoster
Row*, 1898)

Reprinted 1973 by
AUGUSTUS M. KELLEY PUBLISHERS
Reprints of Economic Classics
Clifton New Jersey 07012

Library of Congress Cataloging in Publication Data

Bagehot, Walter, 1826-1877.
    Economic studies.

    (Reprint of economic classics)
    Reprint of the 1898 ed., issued in series: The
Silver library.
    1. Economics--Addresses, essays, lectures. I. Title.
HB171.B14 1973   330   68-55465
ISBN 0-678-00852-3

PRINTED IN THE UNITED STATES OF AMERICA
by SENTRY PRESS, NEW YORK, N. Y. 10013

ECONOMIC STUDIES

BY THE LATE

WALTER BAGEHOT

M.A. AND FELLOW OF UNIVERSITY COLLEGE, LONDON

EDITED BY THE LATE

RICHARD HOLT HUTTON

FOURTH IMPRESSION

LONGMANS, GREEN, AND CO.

39 PATERNOSTER ROW, LONDON

NEW YORK AND BOMBAY

1898

BIBLIOGRAPHICAL NOTE.

Issued in the "Silver Library," *June*, 1895;
reprinted, *June*, 1898.

PREFATORY NOTE TO SECOND EDITION.

SINCE the first edition of this book was published, the two first chapters, which alone received the author's final corrections, have been published separately as a "Students' Edition" for Cambridge undergraduates, with an interesting preface by Professor Marshall. There is, however, so much even in the later and posthumous part of the book which is of permanent value, that a second edition of the complete work is called for, and is now given to the public.

R. H. H.

11th September, 1888.

PREFATORY NOTE TO THE FIRST EDITION.

IT will be obvious to the readers of this book that a considerable portion of it, though hardly to be called fragmentary, is yet not at all as complete as the author, had he lived, would have made it; and that, in the last two essays at all events, there are considerable gaps which he would certainly have filled up. Obviously, too, various other essays would have been added—probably two or three between those which here appear, certainly many on subjects which would naturally have followed the last and least perfect of all the papers, that on "Cost of Production". Indeed Mr. Bagehot is known to have stated that his

economic studies would have worked out into three
distinct volumes, one of which would have been bio-
graphical. Again, no careful reader can fail to perceive that there is a certain amount of redundancy of
statement in these pages, as well as of omission ; and
this was inevitable, for in preparing his finished
writings for the press, the author's practice was to cut
away as well as to add much,—a duty which I was
not imprudent enough to attempt to discharge for him.
Therefore, considering that only the first two essays
had been published, or even printed, in the life-time
of the author, and that, even with the most valuable
help of Mr. Robert Giffen, the head of the Statistical
Department of the Board of Trade (who, during the
last years of Mr. Bagehot's life, had a better knowledge of his economic mind than any other person), I
have had great difficulty in determining the precise
arrangement of some parts of the MS., the folios of
which were often inaccurately numbered, I hope that
the reader may wonder less that much is incomplete,
than that so much that is complete and valuable, as
well as original, remains. No thoughtful economist, I
am sure, who reads this book, will fail to recognise the
value of a great portion of even the least perfect of
these essays.

It only remains for me to express my hearty
gratitude to Mr. Giffen for his willing and most
important help, without which I should have felt no
little hesitation in deciding on the true sequence of
some passages in this volume.

R. H. H.

30th August, 1879.

CONTENTS.

THE POSTULATES

OF

ENGLISH POLITICAL ECONOMY.

ADAM SMITH completed the *Wealth of Nations* in
1776, and our English Political Economy is therefore just a hundred years old.   In that time it has
had a wonderful effect.   The life of almost every
one in England—perhaps of every one—is different
and better in consequence of it.   The whole commercial policy of the country is not so much founded
on it as instinct with it.   Ideas which are paradoxes
everywhere else in the world are accepted axioms
here as results of it.   No other form of political
philosophy has ever had one thousandth part of
the influence on us; its teachings have settled down
into the common sense of the nation, and have
become irreversible.

We are too familiar with the good we have thus
acquired to appreciate it properly.   To do so we
should see what our ancestors were taught.   The best
book on Political Economy published in England
before that of Adam Smith is Sir James Steuart's
Inquiry, a book full of acuteness, and written by a
man of travel and cultivation.   And its teaching is
of this sort: "In all trade two things are to be

considered in the commodity sold. The first is the matter; the second is the labour employed to render this matter useful. The matter exported from a country is what the country loses; the price of the labour exported is what it gains. If the value of the matter imported be greater than the value of what is exported the country gains. If a greater value of labour be imported than exported the country loses. Why? Because in the first case strangers must have paid *in matter* the surplus of labour exported; and in the second place because the strangers must have paid to strangers *in matter* the surplus of labour imported. It is, therefore, a general maxim to discourage the importation of work, and to encourage the exportation of it."[1]

It was in a world where *this* was believed that our present Political Economy began.

Abroad the influence of our English system has of course not been nearly so great as in England itself. But even there it has had an enormous effect. All the highest financial and commercial legislation of the continent has been founded upon it. As curious a testimony perhaps as any to its power is to be found in the memoir of Mollien—the financial adviser of the first Napoleon, *le bon Mollien,* whom nothing would induce him to discard because his administration brought *francs,* whereas that of his more showy competitors might after all end in *ideas.* "It was then," says Mollien, in giving an account of his youth, "that I read an English book

---

[1] Book ii., chap. xxiv.

of which the disciples whom M. Turgot had left
spake with the greatest praise—the work of Adam
Smith. I had especially remarked how warmly the
venerable and judicious Malesherbes used to speak
of it—this book so deprecated by all the men of
the old routine who spoke of themselves so im-
properly as of the school of Colbert. They seemed
to have persuaded themselves that the most important thing for our nation was that not one *sou* should
ever leave France ; that so long as this was so, the
kind and the amount of taxation, the rate of wages,
the greater or less perfection of industrial arts, were
things of complete indifference, provided always that
one Frenchman gained what another Frenchman
lost."

And he describes how the *Wealth of Nations* led
him to abandon those absurdities and to substitute
the views with which we are now so familiar, but
on which the "good Mollien" dwells as on new
paradoxes. In cases like this, one instance is worth
a hundred arguments. We see in a moment the
sort of effect that our English Political Economy
has had when we find it guiding the finance of
Napoleon, who hated ideologues, and who did not
love the English.

But notwithstanding these triumphs, the position
of our Political Economy is not altogether satisfactory. It lies rather dead in the public mind.
Not only does it not excite the same interest as
formerly, but there is not exactly the same confidence in it. Younger men either do not study it,
or do not feel that it comes home to them, and that

it matches with their most living ideas. New sciences have come up in the last few years with new modes of investigation, and they want to know what is the relation of economic science, as their fathers held it, to these new thoughts and these new instruments. They ask, often hardly knowing it, will this "science," as it claims to be, harmonise with what we now know to be sciences, or bear to be tried as we now try sciences? And they are not sure of the answer.

Abroad, as is natural, the revolt is more avowed. Indeed, though the Political Economy of Adam Smith penetrated deep into the continent, what has been added in England since has never penetrated equally; though if our "science" is true, the newer work required a greater intellectual effort, and is far more complete as a scientific achievement than anything which Adam Smith did himself. Political Economy, as it was taught by Ricardo, has had in this respect much the same fate as another branch of English thought of the same age, with which it has many analogies—jurisprudence as it was taught by Austin and Bentham; it has remained insular. I do not mean that it was not often read and understood; of course it was so, though it was often misread and misunderstood. But it never at all reigned abroad as it reigns here; never was really fully accepted in other countries as it was here where it arose. And no theory, economic or political, can now be both insular and secure; foreign thoughts come soon and trouble us; there will always be doubt here as to what is only believed here.

There are, no doubt, obvious reasons why English Political Economy should be thus unpopular out of England. It is known everywhere as the theory "of Free-trade," and out of England Free-trade is almost everywhere unpopular. Experience shows that no belief is so difficult to create, and no one so easy to disturb. The Protectionist creed rises like a weed in every soil. "Why," M. Thiers was asked, "do you give these bounties to the French sugar refiners?" "I wish," replied he, "the tall chimneys to smoke." Every nation wishes prosperity for some conspicuous industry. At what cost to the consumer, by what hardship to less conspicuous industries, that prosperity is obtained, it does not care. Indeed, it hardly knows, it will never read, it will never apprehend the refined reasons which prove those evils and show how great they are ; the visible picture of the smoking chimneys absorbs the whole mind. And, in many cases, the eagerness of England in the Free-trade cause only does that cause harm. Foreigners say : "Your English traders are strong and rich; of course you wish to under-sell our traders, who are weak and poor. You have invented this Political Economy to enrich yourselves and ruin us; we will see that you shall not do so."

And that English Political Economy is more opposed to the action of Government in all ways than most such theories, brings it no accession of popularity. All Governments like to interfere ; it elevates their position to make out that they can cure the evils of mankind. And all zealots wish they should interfere, for such zealots think they can and may convert the rulers and manipulate the State control: it is a distinct object to convert a definite man, and if he will not be convinced there is always a hope of his successor. But most zealots dislike to appeal to the mass of mankind; they know instinctively that it will be too opaque and impenetrable for them.

Still I do not believe that these are the only reasons why our English Political Economy is not estimated at its value abroad. I believe that this arises from its special characteristic, from that which constitutes its peculiar value, and, paradoxical as it may seem, I also believe that this same characteristic is likewise the reason why it is often not thoroughly understood in England itself. The science of Political Economy as we have it in England may be defined as the science of business, such as business is in large productive and trading communities. It is an analysis of that world so familiar to many Englishmen—the "great commerce" by which England has become rich. It assumes the principal facts which make that commerce possible, and as is the way of an abstract science it isolates and simplifies them; it detaches them from the confusion with which they are mixed in fact. And it deals too with the men who carry on that commerce, and who make it possible. It assumes a sort of human nature such as we see everywhere around us, and again it simplifies that human nature; it looks at one part of it only. Dealing with matters of "business," it assumes that man is actuated only by motives of business. It assumes that every man who makes anything, makes it for money, that he always makes that which brings him in most at least cost, and that he will make it in the way that will produce most and spend least; it assumes that every man who buys, buys with his whole heart, and that he who sells, sells with his whole heart, each wanting to gain all possible advantage. Of course we know that this is not so, that men are not like this; but we assume it for simplicity's sake, as an hypothesis. And this deceives many excellent people, for from deficient education they have very indistinct ideas what an abstract science is.

More competent persons, indeed, have understood that English Political Economists are not speaking of real men, but of imaginary ones; not of men as we see them, but of men as it is convenient to us to suppose they are. But even they often do not understand that the world which our Political Economists treat of, is a very limited and peculiar world also. They often imagine that what they read is applicable to all states of society, and to all equally, whereas it is only true of—and only proved as to—states of society in which commerce has largely developed, and where it has taken the form of development, or something near the form, which it has taken in England.

This explains why abroad the science has not been well understood. Commerce, as we have it in England, is not so full-grown anywhere else as it is here—at any rate, is not so outside the lands populated by the Anglo-Saxon race. Here it is not only a thing definite and observable, but about the most definite thing we have, the thing which it is most difficult to help seeing. But on the continent, though there is much that is like it, and though that much is daily growing more, there is nowhere the same pervading entity—the same patent, pressing, and unmistakable object.

And this brings out too the inherent difficulty of the subject—a difficulty which no other science, I think, presents in equal magnitude. Years ago I heard Mr. Cobden say at a league meeting that " Political Economy was the highest study of the human mind, for that the physical sciences required by no means so hard an effort ". An orator cannot be expected to be exactly precise, and of course Political Economy is in no sense the highest study of the mind—there are others which are much higher, for they are concerned with things much nobler than wealth or money ; nor is it true that the effort of mind which Political Economy requires is nearly as great as that required for the abstruser theories of physical science, for the theory of gravitation, or the theory of natural selection ; but, nevertheless, what Mr. Cobden meant had—as was usual with his first-hand mind—a great fund of truth. He meant that Political Economy—effectual Political Economy, Political Economy which in complex problems succeeds—is a very difficult thing ; something altogether more abstruse and difficult, as well as more conclusive, than that which many of those who rush in upon it have a notion of. It is an abstract science which labours under a special hardship. Those who are conversant with its abstractions are usually without a true contact with its facts; those who are in contact with its facts have usually little sympathy with and little cognisance of its abstractions. Literary men who write about it are constantly using what a great teacher calls " unreal words "—that is, they are using expressions with which they have no complete vivid picture to correspond. They are like physiologists who have never dissected; like astronomers who have never seen the stars ; and, in consequence, just when they seem to be reasoning at their best, their knowledge of the facts falls short. Their primitive picture fails them, and their deduction altogether misses the mark—sometimes, indeed, goes astray so far that those who live and move among the facts boldly say that they cannot comprehend " how any one can talk such nonsense ". Yet, on the other hand, these people who live and move among the facts often, or mostly, cannot of themselves put together any precise reasonings about them. Men of business have a solid judgment—a wonderful guessing power of what is going to happen—each in his own trade ; but they have never practised them-selves in reasoning out their judgments and in supporting their guesses by argument : probably if they did so some of the finer and correcter parts of their anticipations would vanish. They are like the sensible lady to whom Coleridge said : " Madam, I accept your conclusion, but you must let me find the logic for it ". Men of business can no more put into words much of what guides their life than they could tell another person how to speak their language. And so the " theory of business " leads a life of obstruction, because theorists do not see the business and the men of business will not reason out the theories.   Far from wondering that such a science is not completely perfect, we should rather wonder that it exists at all.

Something has been done to lessen the difficulty by statistics.   These give tables of facts which help theoretical writers and keep them straight, but the cure is not complete.   Writers without experience of trade are always fancying that these tables mean something more than, or something different from, that which they really mean.   A table of prices, for example, seems an easy and simple thing to understand, and a whole literature of statistics assumes that simplicity ; but in fact there are many difficulties. At the outset there is a difference between the men of theory and the men of practice.   Theorists take a table of prices as facts settled by unalterable laws ; a stockbroker will tell you such prices can be " made".   In actual business such is his constant expression.   If you ask him what is the price of such a stock, he will say, if it be a stock at all out of the common : " I do not know, sir : I will go on to the market and get them to *make* me a price ".   And the following passage from the Report of the late Foreign Loans Committee shows what sort of process " making " a price sometimes is : " Immediately," they say, " after the publication of the prospectus " —the case is that of the Honduras Loan—"and before any allotment was made, M. Lefevre authorised extensive purchases and sales of loans on his behalf ; brokers were employed by him to deal in the manner best calculated to maintain the price of the stock ; the brokers so employed instructed jobbers to purchase the stock when the market required to be strengthened, and to sell it if the market was sufficiently firm. In consequence of the market thus created dealings were carried on to a very large amount. Fifty or a hundred men were in the market dealing with each other and the brokers all round. One jobber had sold the loan (£2,500,000) once over."

Much money was thus abstracted from credulous rural investors ; and I regret to say that book statists are often equally, though less hurtfully, deceived. They make tables in which artificial prices run side by side with natural ones ; in which the price of an article like Honduras scrip, which can be indefinitely manipulated, is treated just like the price of consols, which can scarcely be manipulated at all. In most cases it never occurs to the maker of the table that there could be such a thing as an artificial—a *malâ fide*—price at all. He imagines all prices to be equally straightforward. Perhaps, however, this may be said to be an unfair sample of price difficulties, because it is drawn from the Stock Exchange, the most complex market for prices ; and no doubt the Stock Exchange has its peculiar difficulties, of which I certainly shall not speak lightly; but on the other hand, in one cardinal respect, it is the simplest of markets. There is no question in it of the physical quality of commodities : one Turkish bond of 1858 is as good or bad as another; one ordinary share in a railway exactly the same as any other ordinary share ; but in other markets each

sample differs in quality, and it is a learning in each
market to judge of qualities, so many are they, and
so fine their gradations. Yet mere tables do not tell
this, and cannot tell it. Accordingly in a hundred
cases you may see "prices" compared as if they
were prices of the same thing, when, in fact, they
are prices of different things. The *Gazette* average
of corn is thus compared incessantly, yet it is hardly
the price of the same exact quality of corn in any
two years. It is an average of all the prices in all
the sales in all the markets. But this year the kind
of corn mostly sold may be very superior, and last
year very inferior—yet the tables compare the two
without noticing the difficulty. And when the range
of prices runs over many years, the figures are even
more treacherous, for the names remain, while the
quality, the thing signified, is changed. And of this
persons not engaged in business have no warning.
Statistical tables, even those which are most elaborate
and careful, are not substitutes for an actual cognisance of the facts : they do not, as a rule, convey
a just idea of the movements of a trade to persons
not *in* the trade.

It will be asked, why do you frame such a science
if from its nature it is so difficult to frame it ? The
answer is that it is necessary to frame it, or we must
go without important knowledge. The facts of
commerce, especially of the great commerce, are very
complex. Some of the most important are not on
the surface ; some of those most likely to confuse *are*
on the surface. If you attempt to solve such problems
without some apparatus of method, you are as sure

to fail as if you try to take a modern military fortress
—a Metz or a Belfort—by common assault ; you
must have guns to attack the one, and method to
attack the other.

The way to be sure of this is to take a few new
problems, such as are for ever presented by investigation and life, and to see what by mere common sense
we can make of them.   For example, it is said that
the general productiveness of the earth is less or
more in certain regular cycles, corresponding with
perceived changes in the state of the sun,—what
would be the effect of this cyclical variation in the
efficiency of industry upon commerce?   Some hold,
and as I think hold justly, that, extraordinary as it
may seem, these regular changes in the sun have
much to do with the regular recurrence of difficult
times in the money market.   What common sense
would be able to answer these questions ?   Yet we
may be sure that if there be a periodical series of
changes in the yielding power of this planet, that
series will have many consequences on the industry
of men, whether those which have been suggested or
others.

Or to take an easier case, who can tell without
instruction what is likely to be the effect of the new
loans of England to foreign nations?   We press
upon half-finished and half-civilised communities incalculable sums ; we are to them what the London
money-dealers are to students at Oxford and Cambridge.   We enable these communities to read in
every newspaper that they can have ready money,
almost of any amount, on "personal security".   No

incipient and no arrested civilisations ever had this facility before. What will be the effect on such civilisations now, no untutored mind can say.

Or again : since the Franco-German War an immense sum of new money has come to England; England has become the settling-place of international bargains much more than it was before; but whose mind could divine the effect of such a change as this, except it had a professed science to help it ?

There are indeed two suggested modes of investigation, besides our English Political Economy, and competing with it. One is the Enumerative, or if I may coin such a word, the " all-case method ". One school of theorists say, or assume oftener than they say, that you should have a " complete experience "; that you should accumulate all the facts of these subjects before you begin to reason. A very able German writer has said, in the *Fortnightly Review*,[1] of a great economic topic, banking: " I venture to suggest that there is but one way of arriving at such knowledge and truth "—that is, absolute truth and full knowledge—" namely, a thorough investigation of the facts of the case. By the facts, I mean not merely such facts as present themselves to so-called practical men in the common routine of business, but the facts which a complete historical and statistical inquiry would develop. When such a work shall have been accomplished, German economists may boast of having restored

[1] Gustav Cohn, in the *Fortnightly Review* for September, 1873.

the principles of banking, that is to say, of German banking, but not even then of banking in general. To set forth principles of banking in general, it will be necessary to master in the same way the facts of English, Scotch, French, and American banking—in short, of every country where banking exists." "The only," he afterwards continues, "but let us add also, the safe ground of hope for Political Economy is, following Bacon's exhortation to recommence afresh the whole work of economic inquiry. In what condition would chemistry, physics, geology, zoology, be, and the other branches of natural science which have yielded such prodigious results, if their students had been linked to their chains of deduction from the assumptions and speculations of the last century?"

But the reply is that the method which Mr. Cohn suggests was tried in physical science and failed. And it is very remarkable that he should not have remembered it as he speaks of Lord Bacon, for the method which he suggests is exactly that which Lord Bacon himself followed, and owing to the mistaken nature of which he discovered nothing. The investigation into the nature of heat in the *Novum Organum* is exactly such a collection of facts as Mr. Cohn suggests,—but nothing comes of it. As Mr. Jevons well says: "Lord Bacon's notion of scientific method was that of a kind of scientific book-keeping. Facts were to be indiscriminately gathered from every source, and posted in a kind of ledger from which would emerge in time a clear balance of truth. It is difficult to imagine a less likely way of arriving at discoveries." And yet it is precisely that from which, mentioning Bacon's name, but not forewarned by his experience, Mr. Cohn hopes to make them.

The real plan that has answered in physical science is much simpler. The discovery of a law of nature is very like the discovery of a murder. In the one case you arrest a suspected person, and in the other you isolate a suspected cause. When Newton, by the fall of the apple, or something else, was led to think that the attraction of gravitation would account for the planetary motions, he took that cause by itself, traced out its effects by abstract mathematics, and, so to say, found it "guilty,"—he discovered that it would produce the phenomenon under investigation. In the same way geology has been revolutionised in our own time by Sir Charles Lyell. He for the first time considered the effects of one particular set of causes by themselves. He showed how large a body of facts could be explained on the hypothesis "that the forces now operating upon and beneath the earth's surface are the same both in kind and degree as those which, at remote epochs, have worked out geological changes". He did not wait to begin his inquiry till his data about all kinds of strata, or even about any particular kind, were complete; he took palpable causes as he knew them, and showed how many facts they would explain; he spent a long and most important life in fitting new facts into an abstract and youthful specu- lation. Just so in an instance which has made a literature and gone the round of the world. Mr. Dar- win, who is a disciple of Lyell, has shown how one *vera causa*, "natural selection," would account for an immense number of the facts of nature; for how many, no doubt, is controverted, but, as is admitted, for a very large number. And this he showed by very difficult pieces of reasoning which very few persons would have thought of, and which most people found at first not at all easy to comprehend. The process by which physical science has become what it is, has not been that of discarding abstract speculations, but of working out abstract speculations. The most important known laws of nature —the laws of motion—the basis of the figures in the *Nautical Almanack* by which every ship sails —are difficult and abstract enough, as most of us found to our cost in our youth.

There is no doubt a strong tendency to revolt against abstract reasoning. Human nature has a strong "factish" element in it. The reasonings of the Principia are now accepted. But in the beginning they were "mere crotchets of Mr. Newton's"; Flamstead, the greatest astronomical discoverer of his day—the man of facts, *par excellence*—so called them; they have irresistibly conquered; but at first even those most conversant with the matter did not believe them. I do not claim for the conclusions of English Political Economy the same certainty as for the "laws of motion". But I say that the method by which they have been obtained is the same, and that the difference in the success of the two investigations largely comes from this—that the laws of wealth are the laws of a most complex phenomenon which you can but passively observe, and on which you cannot try experiments for science' sake, and that the laws of motion relate to a matter on which you can experiment, and which is comparatively simple in itself.

And to carry the war into the enemy's country, I say also that the method proposed by Mr. Cohn, the "all-case" method, is impossible. When I read the words "all the facts of English banking," I cannot but ask, of what facts is Mr. Cohn thinking? Banking in England goes on growing, multiplying, and changing, as the English people itself goes on growing, multiplying, and changing. The facts of it are one thing to-day and another to-morrow; nor at one moment does any one know them completely. Those who best know many of them will not tell them or hint at them; gradually and in the course of years they separately come to light, and by the time they do so, for the most part, another crop of unknown ones has accumulated. If we wait to reason till the "facts" are complete, we shall wait till the human race has expired. I consider that Mr. Cohn, and those who think with him, are too "bookish" in this matter. They mean by having all the "facts" before them, having all the printed facts, all the statistical tables. But what has been said of Nature is true of commerce. "Nature," says Sir Charles Lyell, "has made it no part of her concern to provide a record of her operations for the use of men;" nor does trade either—only the smallest of fractions of actual transactions is set down, so that investigation can use it. Literature has been called the "fragment of fragments," and in the same way statistics are the "scrap of scraps". In real life scarcely any one knows more than a small part of what his neighbour is doing, and he scarcely makes public any of that little, or of what he does himself. A complete record of commercial facts, or even of one kind of such facts, is the completest of dreams. You might as well hope for an entire record of human conversation.

There is also a second antagonistic method to that of English Political Economy, which, by contrast, I will call the "single-case" method. It is said that you should analyse each group of facts separately—that you should take the panic of 1866 separately, and explain it; or, at any rate, the whole history of Lombard Street separately, and explain it. And this is very good and very important ; but it is no substitute for a preliminary theory. You might as well try to substitute a corollary for the proposition on which it depends. The history of a panic is the history of a confused conflict of many causes ; and unless you know what sort of effect each cause is likely to produce, you cannot explain any part of what happens. It is trying to explain the bursting of a boiler without knowing the theory of steam. Any history of similar phenomena like those of Lombard Street could not be usefully told, unless there was a considerable accumulation of applicable doctrine before existing, You might as well try to write the "life" of a ship making as you went along the theory of naval construction. Clumsy dissertations would run all over the narrative ; and the result would be a perfect puzzle.

I have been careful not to use in this discussion
of methods the phrase which is oftenest used, *viz.*,
the Historical method, because there is an excessive
ambiguity in it.   Sometimes it seems what I have
called the Enumerative, or " all-case " method ;
sometimes the " single-case " method ; a most confusing double meaning, for by the mixture of the
two, the mind is prevented from seeing the defects
of either.   And sometimes it has other meanings,
with which, as I shall show, I have no quarrel,
but rather much sympathy.   Rightly conceived the
historical method is no rival to the abstract method
rightly conceived.   But I shall be able to explain
this better and less tediously at the end of these
papers than I can at the beginning.

This conclusion is confirmed by a curious circumstance.   At the very moment that our Political
Economy is objected to in some quarters as too
abstract, in others an attempt is made to substitute
for it one which is more abstract still.   Mr. Stanley
Jevons, and M. Walras, of Lausanne, without com-
munication and almost simultaneously, have worked
out a "mathematical" theory of Political Economy ;—
and any one who thinks what is ordinarily taught in
England objectionable, because it is too little concrete in its method, and looks too unlike life and
business, had better try the new doctrine, which he
will find to be much worse on these points than the
old.

But I shall be asked, Do you then say that English
Political Economy is perfect ?—surely it is contrary
to reason that so much difficulty should be felt in

accepting a real science properly treated? At the first beginning no doubt there are difficulties in gaining a hearing for all sciences, but English Political Economy has long passed out of its first beginning? Surely, if there were not some intrinsic defect, it would have been firmly and coherently established, just as others are?

In this reasoning there is evident plausibility, and I answer that, in my judgment, there are three defects in the mode in which Political Economy has been treated in England, which have prevented people from seeing what it really is, and from prizing it at its proper value.

First,—It has often been put forward, not as a theory of the principal causes affecting wealth in *certain* societies, but as a theory of the principal, sometimes even of all, the causes affecting wealth in *every* society. And this has occasioned many and strong doubts about it. Travellers fresh from the sight, and historians fresh from the study, of peculiar and various states of society, look with dislike and disbelief on a single set of abstract propositions which claim, as they think, to be applicable to all such societies, and to explain a most important part of most of them. I cannot here pause to say how far particular English Economists have justified this accusation; I only say that, taking the whole body of them, there is much ground for it, and that in almost every one of them there is some ground. No doubt almost every one—every one of importance— has admitted that there is a "friction" in society which counteracts the effect of the causes treated of.

But in general they leave their readers with the idea
that, after all, this friction is but subordinate; that
probably in the course of years it may be neglected;
and, at any rate, that the causes assigned in the
science of Political Economy, as they treat it, are the
main and principal ones. Now I hold that these
causes are only the main ones in a single kind of
society—a society of grown-up competitive commerce,
such as we have in England; that it is only in such
societies that the other and counteracting forces can
be set together under the minor head of " friction ";
but that in other societies these other causes—in
some cases one, and in some another—are the most
effective ones, and that the greatest confusion arises
if you try to fit on *un*-economic societies the theories
only true of, and only proved as to, economic ones.
In my judgment, we need—not that the authority
of our Political Economy should be impugned, but
that it should be *minimised ;* that we should realise
distinctly where it is established, and where not;
that its sovereignty should be upheld, but its frontiers
marked.   And until this is done, I am sure that there
will remain the same doubt and hesitation in many
minds about the science that there is now.

Secondly,—I think in consequence of this defect
of conception Economists have been far more abstract, and in consequence much more dry, than
they need have been. If they had distinctly set
before themselves that they were dealing only with
the causes of wealth in a single set of societies, they
might have effectively pointed their doctrines with
facts from those societies. But, so long as the

vision of universal theory vaguely floated before them, they shrank from particular illustrations. Real societies are plainly so many and so unlike, that an instance from one kind does not show that the same thing exists in other societies ;—it rather raises in the mind a presumption that it does not exist there ; and therefore speculators aiming at an all-embracing doctrine refrain from telling cases, because those cases are apt to work in unexpected ways, and to raise up the image not only of the societies in which the tenet illustrated is true, but also of the opposite group in which it is false.

Thirdly,—It is also in consequence, as I imagine, of this defective conception of their science, that English Economists have not been as fertile as they should have been in verifying it. They have been too content to remain in the "abstract," and to shrink from concrete notions, because they could not but feel that many of the most obvious phenomena of many nations did not look much like their abstractions. Whereas in the societies with which the science is really concerned, an almost infinite harvest of verification was close at hand, ready to be gathered in ; and because it has not been used, much confidence in the science has been lost, and it is thought "to be like the stars which give no good light because they are so high ".

Of course this reasoning implies that the boundaries of this sort of Political Economy are arbitrary, and might be fixed here or there. But this is already implied when it is said that Political Economy is an abstract science. All abstractions are arbitrary ;

they are more or less convenient fictions made by the mind for its own purposes. An abstract idea means a concrete fact or set of facts *minus* something thrown away. The fact or set of facts were made by nature; but how much you will throw aside of them and how much you will keep for consideration you settle for yourself. There may be any number of political economies according as the subject is divided off in one way or in another, and in this way all may be useful if they do not interfere with one another, or attempt to rule further than they are proved.

The particular Political Economy which I have been calling the English Political Economy, is that of which the first beginning was made by Adam Smith. But what he did was much like the rough view of the first traveller who discovers a country; he saw some great outlines well, but he mistook others and left out much. It was Ricardo who made the first map; who reduced the subjects into consecutive shape, and constructed what you can call a science. Few greater efforts of mind have been made, and not many have had greater fruits. From Ricardo the science passed to a whole set of minds—James Mill, Senior, Torrens, MacCulloch, and others, who busied themselves with working out his ideas, with elaborating and with completing them. For five and twenty years the English world was full of such discussions. Then Mr. J. S. Mill —the Mr. Mill whom the present generation know so well, and who has had so much influence—shaped with masterly literary skill the confused substance

of those discussions into a compact whole. He did
not add a great deal which was his own, and some
of what is due to him does not seem to me of great
value. But he pieced the subjects together, showed
where what one of his predecessors had done had
fitted on to that of another, and adjusted this science
to other sciences according to the notions of that
time. To many students his book is the Alpha and
Omega of Political Economy; they know little of
what was before, and imagine little which can come
after in the way of improvement. But it is not
given to any writer to occupy such a place. Mr.
Mill would have been the last to claim it for himself.
He well knew that, taking his own treatise as the
standard, what he added to Political Economy was
not a ninth of what was due to Ricardo, and that
for much of what is new in his book he was rather
the *Secrétaire de la Rédaction*, expressing and formu-
lating the current views of a certain world, than producing by original thought from his own brain. And
his remoteness from mercantile life, and I should
say his enthusiastic character, eager after things
far less sublunary than money, made him little likely
to give finishing touches to a theory of " the great
commerce ". In fact he has not done so; much yet
remains to be done in it as in all sciences. Mr. Mill,
too, seems to me open to the charge of having
widened the old Political Economy either too much
or not enough. If it be, as I hold, a theory proved
of, and applicable to, particular societies only, much
of what is contained in Mr. Mill's book should not be
there; if it is, on the contrary, a theory holding

good for all societies, as far as they are concerned
with wealth, much more ought to be there, and
much which is there should be guarded and limited.
English Political Economy is not a finished and
completed theory, but the first lines of a great
analysis which has worked out much, but which still
leaves much unsettled and unexplained.

There is nothing capricious, we should observe,
in this conception of Political Economy, nor, though
it originated in England, is there anything specially
English in it.   It is the theory of commerce, as
commerce tends more and more to be when capital
increases and competition grows.   England was the
first—or one of the first—countries to display these
characteristics in such vigour and so isolated as to
suggest a separate analysis of them, but as the world
goes on, similar characteristics are being evolved in one
society after another.   A similar money market, a similar competing trade based on large capital, gradually
tends to arise in all countries.   As " men of the world "
are the same everywhere, so the great commerce is
the same everywhere.   Local peculiarities and ancient
modifying circumstances fall away in both cases;
and it is of this one and uniform commerce which
grows daily, and which will grow, according to every
probability, more and more, that English Political
Economy aspires to be the explanation.

And our Political Economy does not profess to
prove this growing world to be a good world—far
less to be the best.   Abroad the necessity of contesting
socialism has made some writers use the conclusions
brought out by our English science for that object.

But the aim of that science is far more humble; it says these and these forces produce these and these effects, and there it stops. It does not profess to give a moral judgment on either; it leaves it for a higher science, and one yet more difficult, to pronounce what ought and what ought not to be.

The first thing to be done for English Political Economy, as I hold, is to put its aim right. So long as writers on it do not clearly see, and as readers do not at all see, the limits of what they are analysing, the result will not satisfy either. The science will continue to seem what to many minds it seems now, proved perhaps but proved *in nubibus;* true, no doubt, somehow and somewhere, but that somewhere a *terra incognita*, and that somehow an unknown quantity.—As a help in this matter I propose to take the principal assumptions of Political Economy one by one, and to show, not exhaustively, for that would require a long work, but roughly, where each is true and where it is not. We shall then find that our Political Economy is not a questionable thing of unlimited extent, but a most certain and useful thing of limited extent. By marking the frontier of our property we shall learn its use, and we shall have a positive and reliable basis for estimating its value.

I.

THE TRANSFERABILITY OF LABOUR.

THE first assumption which I shall take is that which is perhaps oftener made in our economic reasonings than any other, namely, that labour (masculine labour, I mean) and capital circulate readily within the limits of a nation from employment to employment, leaving that in which the remuneration is smaller and going to that in which it is greater. No assumption can be better founded, as respects such a country as England, in such an economic state as our present one. A rise in the profits of capital, in any trade, brings more capital to it with us now-a-days—I do not say quickly, for that would be too feeble a word, but almost instantaneously. If, owing to a high price of corn, the corn trade on a sudden becomes more profitable than usual, the bill-cases of bill-brokers and bankers are in a few days stuffed with corn bills—that is to say, the free capital of the country is by the lending capitalists, the bankers and bill-brokers, transmitted where it is most wanted. When the price of coal and iron rose rapidly a few years since, so much capital was found to open new mines and to erect new furnaces that the profits of the coal and iron trades have not yet recovered it. In this case the influence of capital attracted by high profits was not only adequate, but much more than adequate : instead of reducing these profits only to an average level, it reduced them below that level; and this happens commonly, for the speculative enterprise which brings in the new capital is a strong, eager, and rushing force, and rarely stops exactly where it should   Here and now a craving for capital in a trade is almost as sure to be followed by a plethora of it as winter to be followed by summer. Labour does not flow so quickly from pursuit to pursuit, for man is not so easily moved as money —but still it moves very quickly.   Patent statistical facts show what we may call "the tides" of our people.   Between the years shown by the last census, the years 1861 and 1871, the population of

The Northern counties increased 23 per cent.			
Yorkshire	,,	19	,,
North-western counties	,,	14	,,
London	,,	16	,,

While that of

The South-western counties only increased 2 per cent.			
Eastern	,,	,,	7	,,
North Midland	,,	,,	9	,,

—though the fertility of marriages is equal.   The set of labour is steadily and rapidly from the counties where there is only agriculture and little to be made of new labour, towards those where there are many employments and where much is to be made of it.

No doubt there are, even at present in England,

many limitations to this tendency, both of capital and of labour, which are of various degrees of importance, and which need to be considered for various purposes. There is a "friction," but still it is only a "friction"; its resisting power is mostly defeated, and at a first view need not be regarded. But taking the world, present and past, as a whole, the exact contrary is true; in most ages and countries this tendency has been not victorious but defeated; in some cases it can scarcely be said even to have existed, much less to have conquered. If you take at random a country in history, the immense chances are that you will find this tendency either to be altogether absent, or not at all to prevail as it does with us now. This primary assumption of our Political Economy is not true everywhere and always, but only in a few places and a few times.

The truth of it depends on the existence of conditions which, taken together, are rarely satisfied. Let us take labour first, as it is the older and simpler of the two. First, there must be "employments," between which labour is to migrate; and this is not true at all of the primitive states of society. We are used to a society which abounds in felt wants that it can satisfy, and where there are settled combinations of men—trades as we call them—each solely occupied in satisfying some one of them. But in primitive times nothing at all like this exists. The conscious wants of men are few, the means of supplying them still fewer, and the whole society homogeneous—one man living much as another.

Civilisation is a shifting mixture of many colours, but barbarism was and is of a dull monotony, hardly varying even in shade.

A picture or two of savage tribes brings this home to the mind better than abstract words. Let us hear Mr. Catlin's description of a favourite North American tribe, with which he means us to be much pleased: "The Mandans, like all other tribes, live lives of idleness and leisure, and of course devote a great deal of time to their amusements, of which they have a great variety. Of these dancing is one of the principal, and may be seen in a variety of forms: such as the buffalo dance, the boasting dance, the begging dance, the scalp dance, and a dozen other dances, all of which have their peculiar characters and meanings and objects." [1]

Then he describes the "starts and jumps" of these dances, and goes on: "Buffaloes, it is well known, are a sort of roaming creatures congregating occasionally in huge masses, and strolling away about the country from east to west or from north to south, or just where their whims or fancies may lead them; and the Mandans are sometimes by this means most unceremoniously left without anything to eat, and being a small tribe and unwilling to risk their lives by going far from home in the face of their more powerful enemies, are oftentimes left almost in a state of starvation. In any emergency of this kind every man musters and brings out of his lodge his mask (the skin of a buffalo's head with

[1] *North American Indians*, Letter 18.

the horns on), which he is obliged to keep in readiness for the occasion; and then commences the
buffalo dance of which I have spoken, which is held
for the purpose of making 'buffalo come,' as they
term it,—of inducing the buffalo herds to change
the direction of their wanderings, and bend their
course towards the Mandan village and graze about
on the beautiful hills and bluffs in its vicinity, where
the Mandans can shoot them down and cook them
as they want them for food. For the most part of
the year the young warriors and hunters by riding
out a mile or two from the village can kill meat in
abundance; and sometimes large herds of these animals may be seen grazing in full view of the village.
There are other seasons also when the young men have
ranged about the country, as far as they are willing to
risk their lives on account of their enemies, without
finding meat. This sad intelligence is brought back
to the chiefs and doctors, who sit in solemn council
and consult on the most expedient measures to be
taken until they are sure to decide the old and only
expedient 'which has never failed'. This is the
buffalo dance, which is incessantly continued till
'buffalo come,' and which the whole village by
relays of dancers keeps up in succession. And when
the buffaloes are seen, there is a brisk preparation
for the chase—a great hunt takes place. The
choicest pieces of the carcase are sacrificed to
the Great Spirit, and then a surfeit or a carouse.
These dances have sometimes been continued for
two or three weeks until the joyful moment when
buffaloes made their appearance. And so they

'*never fail,*' as the village thinks, to bring the buffaloes in."

Such is the mode of gaining the main source of existence, without which the tribe would starve. And as to the rest we are told: "The principal occupations of the women in this village consist in procuring wood and water, in cooking, dressing robes and other skins, in drying meat and wild fruits, and raising maize". [1]

In this attractive description there is hardly any mention of male labour at all; the men hunt, fight, and amuse themselves, and the women do all the rest.

And in the lowest form of savage life, in the stone age, the social structure must have been still more uniform, for there were still less means to break or vary it. The number of things which can be made with a flint implement is much greater than one would have imagined, and savages made more things with it than any one would make now. Time is nothing in the savage state, and protracted labour, even with the worst instrument, achieves much, especially when there are no other means of achieving anything. But there is no formal division of employments— no cotton trade, no iron trade, no woollen trade. There are beginnings of a division, of course, but, as a rule, every one does what he can at everything.

In much later times the same uniformity in the structure of society still continues. We all know

[1] Letter 17.

from childhood how simple is the constitution of a pastoral society. As we see it in the Pentateuch it consists of one family, or a group of families, possessing flocks and herds, on which, and by which, they live. They have no competing employments; no alternative pursuits. What manufactures there are, are domestic, are the work of women at all times, and of men, of certain men, at spare times. No circulation of labour is then conceivable, for there is no circle; there is no group of trades round which to go, for the whole of industry is one trade.

Many agricultural communities are exactly similar. The pastoral communities have left the life of movement, which is essential to a subsistence on the flocks and herds, and have fixed themselves on the soil. But they have hardly done more than change one sort of uniformity for another. They have become peasant proprietors—combining into a village, and holding more or less their land in common, but having no pursuit worth mentioning, except tillage. The whole of their industrial energy—domestic clothes-making and similar things excepted—is absorbed in that.

No doubt in happy communities a division of labour very soon and very naturally arises, and at first sight we might expect that with it a circulation of labour would begin too. But an examination of primitive society does not confirm this idea; on the contrary, it shows that a main object of the social organisation which then exists, is to impede or prevent that circulation. And upon a little thought the reason is evident. There is no paradox in the notion; early nations were not giving up an advantage which they might have had; the good which we enjoy from the circulation of labour was unattainable by them; all they could do was to provide a substitute for it—a means of enjoying the advantages of the division of labour without it,—and this they did. We must carry back our minds to the circumstances of primitive society before we can comprehend the difficulty under which they laboured, and see how entirely it differs from any which we have to meet now.

A free circulation of labour from employment to employment involves an incessant competition between man and man, which causes constant quarrels,—some of which, as we see in the daily transactions of trades unions, easily run into violence; and also a constant series of new bargains, one differing from another, some of which are sure to be broken, or said to be so, which makes disputes of another kind. The peace of society was exposed in early times to greater danger from this source than now, because the passions of men were then less under control than now. " In the simple and violent times," as they have been well called, " which we read of in our Bibles," people struck one another, and people killed one another, for very little matters as we should think them. And the most efficient counteractive machinery which now preserves that peace, then did not exist. We have now in the midst of us a formed, elaborate, strong government, which is incessantly laying down the best rules which it can find to prevent trouble under changing circumstances, and

which constantly applies a sharp pervading force
running through society to prevent and punish
breaches of those rules.   We are so familiar with
the idea of a government inherently possessing and
daily exercising both executive and legislative power,
that we scarcely comprehend the possibility of a
nation existing without them.   But if we attend to
the vivid picture given in the Book of Judges of
an early stage in Hebrew society, we shall see
that there was then absolutely no legislative power,
and only a faint and intermittent executive power.
The idea of law making, the idea of making new
rules for new circumstances, would have been as
incomprehensible to Gideon or Abimelech as the
statutes at large to a child of three years old.
They and their contemporaries thought that there
was an unalterable law consecrated by religion and
confirmed by custom, which they had to obey, but
they could not have conceived an alteration of it
except as an act of wickedness — a worshipping
of Baal.   And the actual coercive power available
for punishing breaches of it was always slight, and
often broken.   One "judge," or ruler, arises after
another, sometimes in one tribe and place, and
sometimes in another, and exercises some kind of
jurisdiction, but his power is always limited ; there
is no organisation for transmitting it, and often there
is no such person—no king in Israel whatever.

The names and the details of this book may or
may not be historical, but its spirit is certainly true.
The peace of society then reposed on a confused
sentiment, in which respect for law, as such—at

least law in our usual modern sense—was an inconsiderable element, and of which the main components were a coercive sense of ingrained usage, which kept men from thinking what they had not before thought, and from doing what they had not before done; a vague horror that something, they did not well know what, might happen if they did so; a close religion which filled the air with deities who were known by inherited tradition, and who hated uninherited ways; and a submission to local opinion inevitable when family and tribe were the main props of life,—when there really was " no world without Verona's walls," [1] —when every exile was an outcast, expelled from what was then most natural, and scarcely finding an alternative existence.

No doubt this sentiment was in all communities partially reinforced by police. Even at the time of the " Judges," there were no doubt " local authorities," as we should now say, who forcibly maintained some sort of order, even when the central power was weakest. But the main support of these authorities was the established opinion; they had no military to call in, no exterior force to aid them; if the fixed sentiment of the community was not strong enough to aid them, they collapsed and failed. But that fixed sentiment would have been at once weakened, if not destroyed, by a free circulation of labour, which is a spring of progress that is favourable to new ideas, that brings in new inventions, that prevents the son being where his father was, that

---

[1] " Romeo and Juliet," iii., 3.

interrupts the traditions of generations and breaks inherited feeling. Besides causing new sorts of quarrels by creating new circumstances and new occasions, this change of men from employment to employment decomposes the moral authority which alone in this state of society can prevent quarrels or settle them. Accordingly, the most successful early societies have forbidden this ready change as much as possible, and have endeavoured, as far as they could, to obtain the advantages of the division of labour without it. Sir Henry Maine to whom this subject so peculiarly belongs, and who has taught us so much more on it than any one else, shall describe the industrial ex· pedients of primitive society as he has seen them still surviving in India. "There is," he says, "yet another feature of the modern Indian cultivating group which connects them with primitive Western communities of the same kind. I have several times spoken of them as organised and self-acting. They, in fact, include a nearly complete establishment of occupations and trades for enabling them to continue their collective life without assistance from any person or body external to them. Besides the headmen or council, exercising quasi-judicial, quasi-legislative power, they contain a village police, now recognised and paid in certain provinces by the British Government. They include several families of hereditary traders; the blacksmith, the harness-maker, the shoemaker. The Brahman is also found for the performance of ceremonies, and even the dancing-girl for attendance at festivities. There is invariably a village accountant, an important person among an unlettered population, so important, indeed, and so conspicuous, that, according to reports current in India, the earliest English functionaries engaged in settlements of land were occasionally led, by their assumption that there must be a single proprietor somewhere, to mistake the accountant for the owner of the village, and to record him as such in the official register. But the person practising any one of these hereditary employments is really a servant of the community as well as one of its component members. He is sometimes paid by an allowance in grain, more generally by the allotment to his family of a piece of land in hereditary possession. Whatever else he may demand for the wares he produces is limited by a fixed price very rarely departed from."[1]

To no world could the free circulation of labour, as we have it in England, and as we assume it in our Political Economy, be more alien, and in none would it have been more incomprehensible. In this case, as in many others, what seems in later times the most natural organisation is really one most difficult to create, and it does not arise till after many organisations which seem to our notions more complex have preceded it and perished. The village association of India, as Sir Henry Maine describes it, seems a much more elaborate structure, a much more involved piece of workmanship, than a common English village where every one chooses his own

[1] *Village Communities*, Lecture iv.

calling, and where there are no special rules for each person, and where a single law rules all. But in fact our organisation is the more artificial because it presupposes the pervading intervention of an effectual Government—the last triumph of civilisation, and one to which early times had nothing comparable. In expecting what we call simple things from early ages, we are in fact expecting them to draw a circle without compasses, to produce the results of civilisation when they have not attained civilisation.

One instance of this want of simplicity in early institutions, which has, almost more than any other, impaired the free transit of labour, is the complexity of the early forms of landholding. In a future page I hope to say something of the general effects of this complexity, and to compare it with the assumptions as to ownership in land made by Ricardo and others. I am here only concerned with it as affecting the movement of men, but in this respect its effect has been incalculable. As is now generally known, the earliest form of landowning was not individual holding, but tribal owning. In the old contracts of Englishmen with savages nothing was commoner than for the king or chief to sell tracts of land,—and the buyers could not comprehend that according to native notions he had no right to do so, that he could not make a title to it, and that according to those notions there was no one who could. Englishmen in all land dealings looked for some single owner, or at any rate some small number of owners, who had an exceptional right over particular pieces of land ; they could not conceive the supposed ownership of a tribe, as in New Zealand, or of a village in India, over large tracts. Yet this joint stock principle is that which has been by far the commonest in the world, and that which the world began with. And not without good reason. In the early ages of society, it would have been impossible to maintain the exclusive ownership of a few persons in what seems at first sight an equal gift to all—a thing to which every one has the same claim. There was then no distinct government apart from and above the tribe any more than among New Zealanders now. There was no compulsory agency which could create or preserve exclusive ownership of the land, even if it wished. And of course it could not have been wished, for though experience has now conclusively shown that such exclusive ownership is desirable for and beneficial to the nation as a whole, as well as to the individual owner, no theorist would have been bold enough to predict this beforehand. This monopoly is almost a paradox after experience, and it would have seemed monstrous folly before it. Indeed, the idea of a discussion of it, is attributing to people in the year 1000 B.C. the notions of people in the year 1800 A.D. Common ownership was then irremediable and inevitable ; no alternative for it was possible, or would then have been conceivable. But it is in its essence opposed to the ready circulation of labour. Few things fix a man so much as a share in a property which is fixed by nature ; and common ownership, wherever it prevails, gives the mass of men such a share.

And there is another force of the same tendency which does not act so widely, but which when it does act is even stronger—in many cases is omnipotent. This is the disposition of many societies to crystallise themselves into *specialised* groups, which are definite units, each with a character of its own, and are more or less strictly hereditary. Sir Henry Maine has described to us how in an Indian village the blacksmith is hereditary, and the harness-maker, and the shoemaker,—and this is natural, for every trade has its secrets, which make a kind of craft or " mystery " of it, and which must be learnt by transmission or not at all. The first and most efficient kind of apprenticeship is that by birth; the father teaches his son that by which he makes his living, almost without knowing it ; the son picks up the skill which is in the air of the house, almost without feeling that he is doing so. Even now we see that there are city families, and university and legal families,—families where a special kind of taste and knowledge are passed on in each generation by tradition, and which in each have in that respect an advantage over others. In most ages most kinds of skilled labour have shown a disposition to intensify this advantage by combination— to form a bounded and exclusive society, guild, trades union, or whatever it may be called, which keeps or tries to keep in each case to itself the rich secret of the inherited art. And even when no pains are taken, each special occupation, after it gains a certain size, tends to form itself into a separate group. Each occupation has certain peculiar characteristics which help to success in it, and which,

therefore, it fosters and develops; and in a subtle
way these traits collect together and form a group-
character analogous to a national character. The
process of caste-making is often thought to be an
old-world thing which came to an end when certain
old castes were made and fixed before the dawn of
history. But in fact the process has been actively
at work in recent times, and has hardly yet died out.
Thus in Cashmere, where the division of castes is
already minute, Mr. Drew tells us that of the Batals
—a class at the very bottom of the scale, "whose
trade it is to remove and skin carcasses, and to cure
leather,"—he has heard " that there are two classes;
so apt are communities in India to divide and to sub-
divide, to perpetuate differences, and to separate
rather than amalgamate. The higher Batals follow
the Mohammedan rules as to eating, and are allowed
some fellowship with the other Mohammedans.
The lower Batals eat carrion, and would not bear
the name of Mohammedans in the mouths of others,
though they might call themselves so."[1] Just so,
Sir W. Hunter says that "the Brahmans of Lower
Bengal bore to the Brahmans of Oudh the same
relation that the landed gentry of Canada or
Australia bears to the landed gentry of England.
Each is an aristocracy, both claim the title of
Esquire, but each is composed of elements whose
social history is widely different, and the home
aristocracy never regards the successful settlers as
equal in rank. The Brahmans of the midland land

[1] *Jummoo and Kashinir Territories*, chap. viii., by Frederick
Drew.

went further; they declared the Brahmans of Lower Bengal inferior not only in the social scale, but in religious capabilities. To this day many of the north country Brahmans do not eat with the Brahmans of the lower valley, and convicted felons from the north-west will suffer repeated floggings in jail, for contumacy, rather than let rice cooked by a Bengal Brahman pass their lips." [1] Caste-making is not a rare act, but a constantly occurring act, when circumstances aid it, and when the human mind is predisposed to it.

One great aid to this process is the mutual animosity of the different groups. "What one nation hates," said Napoleon, "is another nation;" just so, what one caste hates is another caste: the marked characteristics of each form—by their difference—a certain natural basis for mutual dislike. There is an intense disposition in the human mind—as you may see in any set of schoolboys—to hate what is unusual and strange in other people, and each caste supplies those adjoining it with a conspicuous supply of what is unusual. And this hatred again makes each caste more and more unlike the other, for every one wishes as much as possible to distinguish himself from the neighbouring hated castes by excelling in the peculiarities of his own caste, and by avoiding theirs.

In the ancient parts of the world these contrasts of group to group are more or less connected for the most part with contrasts of race. Very often the origin of the caste—the mental tendency which made

---

[1] *Annals of Rural Bengal*, by Sir W. W. Hunter, chap. iii.

its first members take to its special occupation—was some inborn peculiarity of race; and at other times, as successive waves of conquest passed over the country, each race of conquerors connected themselves most with, and at last were absorbed in, the pre-existing kind of persons which they most resembled, and frequently in so doing hardened into an absolute caste what was before a half-joined and incipient group.

Each conquest, too, tends to make a set of outcasts—generally from the worst part of the previous population—and these become "hewers of wood and drawers of water" to the conquerors—that is, they are an outlying and degraded race, which is not admitted to compete or mix with the others, and which becomes more degraded from feeling that it is thus inferior, and from being confined to the harder, baser, and less teaching occupations. And upon these unhappy groups the contempt and hatred of the higher ones tend to concentrate themselves, and, like most strong sentiments in the early world, these feelings find for themselves a religious sanction. To many villages in India, Sir Henry Maine says, there are attached a class of "outsiders" who never enter the village, or only enter reserved portions of it, who are looked on as "essentially impure," "whose very touch is avoided as contaminating". These poor people are more or less thought to be "accursed"; to have some taint which shows that the gods hate them, and which justifies men in hating them too, and in refusing to mix with them.

The result of these causes is, that many ancient

societies are complex pieces of patchwork—bits of contrasted human nature, put side by side. They have a variegated complexity, which modern civilised States mostly want. And there must clearly have been an advantage in this organisation of labour— to speak of it in modern phrase—though it seems to us now so strange, or it would not have sprung up independently in many places and many ages, and have endured in many for long tracts of years. This advantage, as we have seen, was the gain of the division of labour without the competition which with us accompanies it, but which the structure of society was not then hard enough to bear.

No doubt we must not push too far this notion of the rigidity of caste. The system was too rigid to work without some safety-valves, and in every age and place where that system prevails, some have been provided. Thus in India we are told " a Brahmana unable to subsist by his duties may live by the duty of a soldier; if he cannot get a subsistence by either of these employments, he may apply to tillage and attendance on cattle, or gain a competence by traffic, avoiding certain commodities. A Kshatriya in distress may subsist by all these means, but he must not have recourse to the highest functions. A Vaisya unable to subsist by his own duties may descend to the servile acts of a S'údra ; and a S'údra, not finding employment by waiting on men of the higher classes, may subsist by handicrafts ; besides the particular occupations assigned to the mixed classes, they have the alternative of following that profession which regularly belongs to the class from which they derive their origin on the mother's side;"[1] and so on, without end.

And probably it is through these supplementary provisions, as I may call them, that the system of caste ultimately breaks down and disappears. It certainly disappeared in ancient Egypt when the compact Roman Government was strong enough to do without it, and when a change of religion had removed the sanctions which fixed and consecrated it. The process is most slow, as our experience in India proves. The saying that " La providence a ses aises dans le temps" has rarely elsewhere seemed so true. Still, the course is sure, and the caste system will in the end pass away, whenever an efficient substitute has been made for it, and the peace of industry secured without it.

But it would be a great mistake to believe that, whenever and wherever there is an efficient external government capable of enforcing the law, and of making the competitive migration of labour safe and possible, such migration of itself at once begins. There is, in most cases, a long and dreary economic interval to be passed first. In many countries, the beginning of such migration is for ages retarded by the want of another requisite—the want of external security. We have come in modern Europe to look on nations as if they were things indestructible—at least, on large nations. But this is a new idea, and even now it has to be taken with many qualifications. In many periods of history it has not been true at

---

[1] Colebrooke's Essays, vol. ii., No. vi., " Indian Classes ".

all ; the world was in such confusion, that it was
almost an even chance whether nations should
continue, or whether they should be conquered and
destroyed. In such times the whole energy of the
community must be concentrated on its own defence ;
all that interferes with it must be sacrificed, if it is
to live. And the most efficient mode of defending
it is generally a feudal system ; that is, a local
militia based on the land, where each occupier of
the soil has certain services to render, of which
he cannot divest himself, and which he must stay
on certain definite fields to perform when wanted.
In consequence the races of men which were possessed of an organisation easily adapting itself to
the creation of such a militia, have had a striking
tendency to prevail in the struggle of history.
"The feudal system," says Sir George Campbell,
on many accounts one of our most competent
judges, " I believe to be no invention of the Middle
Ages, but the almost necessary result of the hereditary
character of the Indo-Germanic institutions, when
the tribes take the position of dominant conquerors.
They form, in fact, an hereditary army, with that
gradation of fealty from the commander to the
private soldier which is essential in military operations. Accordingly, we find that among all the
tribes of Indo-Germanic blood which have conquered
and ruled Indian provinces, the tendency is to
establish a feudal system extremely similar to that
which prevailed in Europe. In Rajpootana the
system is still in full force. The Mahrattas and
Sikhs had both established a similar system. In

my early days it existed in great perfection in some parts of the Cis-Sutlej States." [1]　And where the system is most developed, at the lowest point of the scale there is always an immovable class—serfs, *villeins regardants*, or what we choose to call them—who do not fight themselves, who perhaps are too abject in spirit, or perhaps are of too dubious fidelity to be let have arms, but who cultivate the ground for those who really fight.　The soldier class, rooted to the land by martial tenure, has beneath it a non-soldier class even more rooted to the soil by the tenure of tilling it.　I need not say how completely such a system of military defence, and such a system of cultivation, are opposed to the free transit of labour from employment to employment.　Where these systems are perfectly developed, this transit is not so much impeded as prevented.

And there is a yet more pervading enemy of the free circulation of labour.　This is slavery.　We must remember that our modern notion that slavery is an exceptional institution, is itself an exceptional idea; it is the product of recent times and recent philosophies.　No ancient philosopher, no primitive community, would have comprehended what we meant by it.　That human beings are divided into strong and weak, higher and lower, or what is thought to be such; and that the weak and inferior ought to be made to serve the higher and better, whether they would wish to do so or not, are settled axioms of early thought.　Whatever might be the origin

[1] "Tenure of Land in India," chap. iii. of *Systems of Land Tenure in Various Countries* (Cobden Club Essays).

and whatever might be the fate of other institutions, the ancient world did not doubt that slavery at all events existed " by the law of nature," and would last as long as men. And it interferes with the ready passage of labour from employment to employment in two ways. First, it prevents what we call for this purpose " employments "—that is, markets where labour may be bought, mostly in order that the produce may be sold. Slavery, on the contrary, strengthens and extends domestic manufactures where the produce is never sold at all, where it is never intended to be so, but where each household by its own hands makes what it wants. In a slave-community so framed, not only is there little quick migration of free labour, but there are few fit places for it to migrate between ; there are no centres for the purchase of much of it ; society tends to be divided into self-sufficing groups, buying little from the exterior. And at a later stage of industrial progress slavery arrests the movement of free labour still more effectively by providing a substitute. It is, then, the slave labour which changes occupation, and not the free labour. Just as in the present day a capitalist who wants to execute any sort of work hires voluntary labour to do it, so in a former stage of progress he would buy slaves in order to do it. He might not, indeed, be able to buy enough slaves— enough suitable slaves, that is, for his purpose. The organisation of slavery has never been as effectual as our present classified system of free labour, and from intrinsic defects never can be. But it does develop earlier. Just when the system of free labour might develop if it were let alone, the imperfect substitute of slavery steps in and spoils it. When free labour still moves slowly and irregularly, and when frequent wars supply the slave-market with many prisoners, the slave-market is much the easiest resource of the capitalist. So it is when a good slave-trade keeps it well filled. The capitalist finds it better to buy than to hire, for there are in this condition of things comparatively many men to be bought and comparatively few to be hired. And the result takes unexpected directions. "What the printing-press is in modern times," says a German writer, "that slavery was in ancient times."   And though this may be a little exaggerated, it is certain that in ancient Rome books were produced much cheaper and in much greater number than they were for hundreds of years afterwards.   When there was a demand for a book, extra copying-slaves could be "turned on" to multiply it in a way which in later times, when slavery had ceased, was impossible, and which is only surpassed by the way in which additional compositors are applied to works in demand now. And political philosophers proposed to obtain revenue from this source, and to save taxation. "Suppose," says Xenophon, "that the Athenian State should buy twelve hundred slaves, and should let them out to work in the mines at an obolus a head, and suppose that the whole amount annually thus received should be employed in the purchase of new slaves, who should again in the same way yield the same income, and so on successively; the State would then by these means in five or six

years possess six thousand slaves," which would
yield a large income.   The idea of a compound
interest investment in men, though abhorrent to us,
seemed most natural to Xenophon.   And almost
every page of the classics proves how completely
the civilisation then existing was based on slavery
in one or other of its forms—that of skilled labour
(the father of Demosthenes owned thirty-three
cutlers and twenty coachmakers) or unskilled, that
might either be worked by the proprietor or let out,
as he liked.   Even if this system had only economic
consequences, it must have prevented the beginning
of freely moving labour, for it is much handier than
such a system can be at its outset.   And as we
know, the system has moral effects working in the
same way even more powerful, for it degrades
labour by making it the slave-mark, and makes the
free labourer — whether the *prolétaire* of ancient
cities, or the "mean white" of American planta-
tions—one ·of the least respectable and the least
workmanlike of mankind.

Happily this full-grown form of slavery is exceedingly frail.   We have ourselves seen in America
how completely it collapses at an extrinsic attack ;
how easy it is to destroy it, how impossible to revive
it.   And much of the weakness of ancient civilisation was also so caused.   Any system which makes
the mass of a society hate the constitution of that
society, must be in unstable equilibrium.   A small
touch will overthrow it, and scarcely any human
power will re-establish it.   And this is the necessary
effect of capitalistic slavery, for it prevents all other

labourers, makes slaves the "many" of the community, and fills their mind with grief and hatred.
Capitalistic slavery is, as history shows, one of the
easiest things to efface, as domestic slavery is one of
the hardest. But capitalistic slavery has vitally
influenced most of the greatest civilisations; and
as domestic slavery has influenced nearly all of
them, the entire effect of the two has been prodigious.

We see then that there are at least four conditions
to be satisfied before this axiom of our English
Political Economy is true within a nation. Before
labour can move easily and as it pleases from employment to employment there must be such employments for it to move between ;—there must be
an effectual government capable of maintaining
peace and order during the transition and not requiring itself to be supported by fixity of station in
society as so many governments have been ;—the
nation must be capable of maintaining its independent existence against other nations without a
military system dependent on localised and immovable
persons ; and there must be no competing system
of involuntary labour limiting the number of employments or moving between them more perfectly than
contemporary free labour. These are not indeed
all the conditions needful for the truth of the axiom,
but the others can be explained better when some
other matters have been first discussed.

II.

THE TRANSFERABILITY OF CAPITAL.

In my last paper I discussed the fundamental
principle of English Political Economy, that within
the limits of a nation labour migrates from employment to employment, as increased remuneration
attracts or decreased remuneration repels it; and
now I have to treat the corresponding principle as to
capital, that it flows or tends to flow to trades of
which the profits are high, that it leaves or tends to
leave those in which the profits are low, and that in
consequence there is a tendency—a tendency limited
and contracted, but still a tendency—to an equality
of profits through commerce.

First, this requires such a development of the
division of labour as to create what we call " trade,"
that is to say, a set of persons working for the wants
of others, and providing for their own wants by the
return-commodities received from those others. But
this development has only been gradually acquired
by the human race. Captain Cook found some
Australian tribes to whom the idea of traffic seemed
unknown. They received what was given them
readily, but they received it as a present only; they
seemed to have no notion of giving anything in lieu
of it. The idea of barter—an idea usually so familiar

to the lower races of men—appeared never to have
dawned on these very low ones. But among races
in such a condition there is no change of trades as
capital becomes more and more profitable in any
one. The very conception comes long after. Every
one works for himself at everything; and he always
works most at what he likes most for the time; as
he changes his desires, so far as he can he changes
his labour. Whenever he works he uses the few
tools he has, the stone implements, the charred wood,
the thongs of hide, and other such things, in the best
way he can; a hundred savages are doing so at once,
some in one way, some in another, and these are
no doubt "shiftings of capital". But there is no
computation of profit, as we now reckon profit, on
such shiftings. Profit, as we calculate, means that
which is over after the capital is replaced. But a
savage incapable of traffic does not make this
calculation as to his flints and his hides. The idea
could not even be explained to him.

Secondly, this comparison requires a medium in
which the profits can be calculated, that is, a *money*.
Supposing that in the flax trade profits are 5 per
cent., and that side by side in the cotton trade they
are 15 per cent., capital will now-a-days immediately
run from one to the other. And it does so because
those who are making much, try to get more capital,
and those who are making little—still more those
who are losing—do not care to keep as much as they
have. But if there is no money to compute in,
neither will know what they are making, and therefore the process of migration wants its motive, and

will not begin. The first sign of extra profit in a trade—not a conclusive, but a strongly presumptive one—is an extra high price in the article that trade makes or sells; but this test fails altogether when there is no " money " to sell in. And the debit side of the account, the cost of production, is as difficult to calculate when there is no common measure between its items, or between the product, and any of them. Political Economists have indeed an idea of " exchangeable value "—that is, of the number of things which each article will exchange for—and they sometimes suppose a state of barter in which people had this notion, and in which they calculated the profit of a trade by deducting the exchangeable value of the labour and commodities used in its production from the value of the finished work. But such a state of society never existed in reality. No nation, which was not clever enough to invent a money, was ever able to conceive so thin and hard an idea as " exchangeable value ". Even now Mr. Fawcett justly says that it puzzles many people, and sends them away frightened from books on Political Economy. In fact it is an ideal which those used to money-prices have framed to themselves. They see that the price of anything, the money it fetches, is equal to its " purchasing power " over things, and by steadily attending they come to be able to think of this " purchasing power " separately, and to call and reason upon it as exchangeable value. But the idea is very treacherous even to skilled minds, and even now-a-days not the tenth part of any population could ever take it in.

As for the nations really in a state of barter ever comprehending it, no one can imagine it, for they are mostly unequal to easy arithmetic, and some cannot count five. A most acute traveller thus describes the actual process of bargaining among savage nations as he saw it. "In practice," Mr. Galton tells us of the Damaras, "whatever they may possess in their language, they certainly use no numeral greater than three. When they wish to express four they take to their fingers, which are to them as formidable instruments of calculation as a sliding-rule is to an English schoolboy. They puzzle very much after five, because no spare hand remains to grasp and secure the fingers that are required for 'units'. Yet they seldom lose oxen: the way in which they discover the loss of one is not by the number of the herd being diminished, but by the absence of a face which they know. When bartering is going on each sheep must be paid for separately. Thus suppose two sticks of tobacco to be the rate of exchange for one sheep, it would sorely puzzle a Damara to take two sheep and give him four sticks. I have done so, and seen a man first put two of the sticks apart, and take a sight over them at one of the sheep he was about to sell. Having satisfied himself that that one was honestly paid for, and finding to his surprise that exactly two sticks remained in hand to settle the account for the other sheep, he would be afflicted with doubts; the transaction seemed too pat to be correct, and he would refer back to the first couple of sticks, and then his mind got hazy and confused, and wandered

from one sheep to the other, and he broke off the
transaction until two sticks were put into his hand
and one sheep driven away, and then the other two
sticks given him, and the second sheep driven away."[1]
Such a delineation of primitive business speaks for
itself, and it is waste of space showing further that
an abstraction like "value in exchange" is utterly
beyond the reach of the real bartering peoples—that
a habit of using money, and of computing in it, are
necessary preliminaries to comparisons of profits.

Unquestionably the most primitive community can
see if a pursuit utterly fails, or if it immensely
succeeds. The earliest men must have been eager
in making flint tools, for there are so many of them,
and no doubt they did not try to breed cattle where
they died. But there was in those days no adjusted
comparison between one thing and another; all
pursuits which anyhow suited went on then as they
do among savages now.

Money, too, is in this matter essential, or all but
essential, in another way. It is a form in which
capital is held *in suspense* without loss. The transfer
of capital from employment to employment is a
matter requiring consideration, consideration takes
time, and the capital must be somewhere during
that time. But most articles are bought at a risk;
they lose in the process, and become second-hand;
an ordinary person cannot get rid of them without
receiving for them less—often much less—than he
gave. But money is never "second-hand"; it will

[1] "*Travels in Tropical South Africa,* by Francis Galton,
chap. v., p. 113.

in any direction. The moment any set of traders want capital, the best of them, those whose promises are well known to be good, get it in a minute, because it is lying ready in the hands of those who know, and who live by knowing, that they are fit to have it.

Secondly,—In modern England, there is a great speculative fund which is always ready to go into anything which promises high profits. The largest part of this is composed of the savings of men of business. When, as in 1871, the profits of many trades suddenly become much greater than usual, the Stock Exchange instantly becomes animated; there is at once a market for all kinds of securities, so long as they promise much, either by great interest or by rise of prices. Men of business who are used to a high percentage of profit in their own trade despise 3 or 4 per cent., and think that they ought to have much more. In consequence there is no money so often lost as theirs; there is an idea that it is the country clergyman and the ignorant widow who mostly lose by bad loans and bad companies. And no doubt they often do lose. But I believe that it is oftener still men of business, of slight education and of active temperament, who have made money rapidly, and who fancy that the skill and knowledge of a special trade which have enabled them to do so, will also enable them to judge of risks, and measure contingencies out of that trade; whereas, in fact, there are no persons more incompetent, for they think they know everything, when they really know almost nothing out of their little busi-

ness, and by habit and nature they are eager to be
doing. So much of their money as comes to London
is in greater jeopardy almost than any other money.
But there is a great deal which never comes there,
and which those who make it are able to put out
in pushing their own trade and in extending allied
trades. The very defects which make the trader
so bad a judge of other things make him an excellent
judge of these, and he is ready and daring, and
most quick to make use of what he knows. Each
trade in modern commerce is surrounded by subsidiary and kindred trades, which familiarise the
imagination with it, and make its state known; as
soon, therefore, as the conspicuous dealers in that
trade are known to be doing particularly well, the
people in the surrounding trades say, " Why should
not we do as well too?" and they embark their
capital in it—sometimes, of course, wrongly, but
upon the whole wisely and beneficially. In an animated business world like ours, these inroads into
the trades with largest gains by the nearest parts
of the speculative fund are incessant, and are a
main means of equalising profits.

Lastly,—There is the obvious tendency of young
men starting in business to go into the best-paying
business, or what is thought to be so at that time.
This, in the best cases, also acts mainly on the
allied and analogous trades. Little good, for the
most part, comes of persons who have been brought
up on one side of the business world going quite to
the other side—of farmers' sons going to cotton-
spinning, or of lacemakers' sons going into shipping.

Each sort of trade has a tradition of its own, which is never written, probably could not be written, which can only be learned in fragments, and which is best taken in early life, before the mind is shaped and the ideas fixed. From all surrounding trades there is an incessant movement of young men with new money into very profitable trades, which steadily tends to reduce that profitableness to the common average.

I am more careful than might seem necessary to describe the entire process of equalisation at length, because it is only by so doing that we can see how complex it is, and how much development in society it requires ; but as yet the description is not complete, or nearly so. We have only got as far as the influx of money into new trades, but this is but a small part of what is necessary. Trades do not live by money alone ; money by itself will not make anything. What, then, do we mean when we speak of " capital " as flowing from employment to employment ?

Some writers speak as if the only thing which transfers of capital effect is a change in the sort of labour that is set in motion ; and no doubt this is so far true, that all new employments of capital do require new labour. Human labour is the primitive moving force, and you must have more of it if you want more things done ; but the description, though true, is most incomplete, as the most obvious facts in the matter prove. When new capital comes into cotton-spinning, this means not only that new money is applied to paying cotton operatives, but also that new money is applied to buying new spinning machines; these spinning machines are made by other machines, as well as labour; and the second lot of machines again by a third set, as well as other labour. In the present state of the world, nothing is made by brute labour; everything is made by aids to labour; and when capital goes from trade to trade, it settles not only which sort of labour shall be employed, but which sort of existing machines shall be first used up, which sort of new ones made, and how soon those new ones shall be worn out, not only in the selected trade, but in an endless series subsidiary to it.

To understand the matter fully, we must have a distinct view of what on this occasion and on this matter we mean by "capital". The necessity of a science like Political Economy is that it mus borrow its words from common life, and therefore from a source where they are not used accurately, and cannot be used accurately. When we come to reason strictly on the subjects to which they relate we must always look somewhat precisely to their meaning and the worst is that it will not do, if you are writing for the mass of men, even of educated men, to use words always in the same sense. Common words are so few, that if you tie them down to one meaning they are not enough for your purpose; they do their work in common life because they are in a state of incessant slight variation; meaning one thing in one discussion and another a little different in the next. If we were really to write an invariable nomenclature in a science where we have so much to say of so many things

as we have in Political Economy, we must invent
new terms, like the writers on other sciences.
Mr. de Morgan said (in defence of some fresh-coined
substantive) : "Mathematics must not want words
because Cicero did not know the differential cal-
culus". But a writer on Political Economy is bound
—not perhaps by Cicero—but by his readers. He
must not use words out of his own head, which they
never heard of; they will not read him if he does.
The best way, as we cannot do this, is to give up
uniform uses—to write more as we do in common
life, where the context is a sort of unexpressed "interpretation clause," showing in what sense words
are used; only, as in Political Economy we have
more difficult things to speak of than in common
conversation, we must take more care, give more
warning of any change, and at times write out the
"interpretation clause" for that page or discussion,
least there should be any mistake. I know that
this is difficult and delicate work; and all I have
to say in defence of it is that in practice it is safer
than the competing plan of inflexible definitions.
Any one who tries to express varied meanings on
complex things with a scanty vocabulary of fastened
senses, will find that his style grows cumbrous without being accurate, that he has to use long peri-
phrases for common thoughts, and that after all
he does not come out right, for he is half his time
falling back into the senses which fit the case in
hand best, and these are sometimes one, sometimes
another, and almost always different from his "hard
and fast" sense. In such discussions we should

learn to vary our definitions as we want, just as we say, "let x, y, z mean" now this, and now that, in different problems; and this, though they do not always avow it, is really the practice of the clearest and most effective writers.

By capital, then, in this discussion, we mean an aggregate of two unlike sorts of artificial commodities —co-operative things which help labour, and re-munerative things which pay for it. The two have this in common, that they are the produce of human labour, but they differ in almost everything else if you judge of them by the visual appearance. Be-tween a loaf of bread and a steam-engine, between a gimlet and a piece of bacon, there looks as if there were really nothing in common, except that man manufactured both. But, though the contrast of externalities is so great, the two have a most essential common property which is that which Political Economy fixes upon; the possible effect of both is to augment human wealth. Labourers work because they want bread; their work goes farther if they have good tools; and therefore economists have a common word for both tools and bread. They are both capital, and other similar things are so too.

And here we come across another of the inevitable verbal difficulties of Political Economy. Taking its words from common life, it finds that at times and for particular discussions it must twist them in a way which common people would never think of. The obvious resemblances which we deal with in life dictate one mode of grouping objects in the mind, and one mode of speaking of them; the latent but more powerful resemblance which science finds would dictate another form of speech and mental grouping. And then what seems a perverse use of language must be made. Thus, for the present discussion, the acquired skill of a labourer is capital, though no one in common life would call it so. It is a productive thing made by man, as much as any tool; it *is*, in fact, an immaterial tool which the labourer uses just as he does a material one. It is co-operative capital as much as anything can be. And then, again, the most unlikely-looking and luxurious articles are capital if they reward and stimulate labour. Artisans like the best of rabbits, the best bits of meat, green peas, and gin; they work to get these; they would stay idle if they were not incited by these, and therefore these are "capital". Political Economy (like most moral sciences) requires not only to change its definitions as it moves from problem to problem, but also for some problems to use definitions which, unless we see the motive, seem most strange; just as in Acts of Parliament the necessity of the draftsman makes a very technical use of words necessary if he is to do his work neatly, and the reader will easily be most mistaken and confused if he does not heed the dictionary which such Acts contain.

Remembering all this, we see at once that it is principally remunerative capital which is transferable from employment to employment. Some tools and instruments are, no doubt, used in many trades, especially the complex ones; knives, hammers, twine, and nails can be used, are used, in a thousand. The

existing stock of these is transferred bodily when
capital migrates from an employment. But, in
general, as I have said before, the effect of the migration on co-operative capital is to change the speed
with which the existing machines are worked out,
and the nature of the new machines which are made;
the "live skill" of an artisan being treated as a
machine. On remunerative capital the effect is
simpler. As a rule, much the same commodities
reward labour in different trades, and if one trade
declines and another rises, the only effect is to
change the labourer who gets these commodities; or,
if the change be from a trade which employs little
skilled labour to one which employs much, then the
costly commodities which skilled labour wants will
be in demand, more of them will be made, and there
will be an increase of animation in all the ancillary
trades which help their making.

We see also more distinctly than before what we
mean by an "employment". We mean a group of
persons with fitting tools and of fitting skill paid by
the things they like. I purposely speak of "tools"
to include all machines, even the greatest, for I want
to fix attention on the fact that everything depends
on the effort of man, on the primary fruit of human
labour. Without this to start with, all else is
useless. And I use it out of brevity to include such
things as coal and materials, which for any other
purpose no one would call so, but which are plainly
the same for what we have now to do with.

And "employment" in any large trade implies an
"employer". The capitalist is the motive power in

modern production, in the "great commerce". He
settles what goods shall be made, and what not;
what brought to market, and what not. He is the
general of the army; he fixes on the plan of operations, organises its means, and superintends its
execution. If he does this well, the business
succeeds and continues; if he does it ill, the business
fails and ceases. Everything depends on the correct-
ness of the unseen decisions, on the secret sagacity
of the determining mind. And I am careful to dwell
on this, though it is so obvious, and though no man
of business would think it worth mentioning, because
books forget it,—because the writers of books are
not familiar with it. They are taken with the con-
spicuousness of the working classes; they hear them
say: "It is we who made Birmingham, we who
made Manchester," but you might as well say that
it was the "compositors" who made the *Times* newspaper. No doubt the craftsmen were necessary to
both, but of themselves they were insufficient to either.
The printers do not settle what is to be printed;
the writers do not even settle what is to be written.
It is the editor who settles everything. He creates
the *Times* from day to day; on his power of hitting
the public fancy its prosperity and power rest;
everything depends on his daily bringing to the
public exactly what the public wants to buy; the
rest of Printing-House Square—all the steam-presses,
all the type, all the staff, clever as so many of them
are,—are but implements which he moves. In the
very same way the capitalist edits the "business";
it is he who settles what commodities to offer

to the public; how and when to offer them, and all the rest of what is material. This monarchical structure of money business increases as society goes on, just as the corresponding structure of war business does, and from the same causes. In primitive times a battle depends as much on the prowess of the best fighting men, of some Hector or some Achilles, as on the good science of the general. But now-a-days it is a man at the far end of a telegraph wire—a Count Moltke, with his head over some papers,—who sees that the proper persons are slain, and who secures the victory. So in commerce. The primitive weavers are separate men with looms apiece, the primitive weapon-makers separate men with flints apiece; there is no organised action, no planning, contriving, or foreseeing in either trade, except on the smallest scale; but now the whole is an affair of money and management; of a thinking man in a dark office, computing the prices of guns or worsteds. No doubt in some simple trades these essential calculations can be verified by several persons—by a board of directors, or something like it. But these trades, as the sagacity of Adam Smith predicted,[1] and as painful experience now shows, are very few; the moment there comes anything difficult or complicated, the Board "does not see its way," and then, except it is protected by a monopoly, or something akin to monopoly, the individual capitalist beats it out of the field. But the details of this are not to my present purpose. The sole point now

[1] *The Wealth of Nations*, book v., chap. i

material is that the transference of capital from employment to employment involves the pre-existence of employment, and this pre-existence involves that of " employers ": of a set of persons—one or many, though usually one—who can effect the transfer of that capital from employment to employment, and can manage it when it arrives at the employment to which it is taken.

And this management implies knowledge. In all cases successful production implies the power of adapting means to ends, of making what you want as you want it. But after the division of labour has arisen, it implies much more than this: it then requires, too, that the producer should know the wants of the consumer, a man whom mostly he has never seen, whose name probably he does not know, very likely even speaking another language, living according to other habits, and having scarcely any point of intimate relation to the producer, except a liking for what he produces. And if a person who does not see is to suit another who is not seen, he must have much head-knowledge, an acquired learning in strange wants as well as of the mode of making things to meet them. A person possessing that knowledge is necessary to the process of transferring capital, for he alone can use it when the time comes, and if he is at the critical instant not to be found, the change fails, and the transfer is a loss and not a gain.

This description of the process by which capital is transferred and of what we mean by it, may seem long, but it will enable us to be much shorter in showing the conditions which that transfer implies. First, it presupposes the existence of transferable labour, and I showed before how rare transferable labour is in the world, and how very peculiar are its prerequisites. You cannot have it unless you have a strong government, which will keep peace in the delicate line on which people are moving. You must not have fixed castes in inherited occupations, which at first are ways and means to do without a strong government, but which often last on after it begins; you must not have a local army which roots men to fixed spots for military purposes, and therefore very much to fixed pursuits; and you must not have slavery, for this is an imperfect substitute for free transferable labour, which effectually prevents the existence of it. Complete freedom of capital pre-supposes complete freedom of labour, and can only be attained when and where this exists.

No doubt capital begins to move much before the movement of labour is perfect. The first great start of it commences with a very unpopular person, who is almost always spoken evil of when his name is mentioned, but in whom those who know the great things of which he has been the forerunner will always take a great interest. It is the money-lender in a primitive community, whose capital is first transferred readily from occupation to occupation. Suppose a new crop, say cotton, becomes suddenly lucrative, immediately the little proprietors throng to the money-lender's to obtain funds to buy cotton. A new trade is begun by his help, which could not have been begun without him. If cotton ceases to be a good crop, he ceases to lend to grow it, his spare capital either remains idle or goes to some other loan, perhaps to help some other crop which has taken the place of cotton in profitableness. There is no more useful trade in early civilisation, though there is none which has such a bad name, and not unnaturally, for there is none which then produces more evil as well as good. Securities for loans, such as we have them in developed commerce, are rarely to be met with in early times ; the land —the best security as we think it—is then mostly held upon conditions which prevent its being made in that way available ; there is little moveable property of much value, and peasants who work the land have scarcely any of that little; the only thing they can really pledge is their labour—*themselves.* But then when the loan is not paid, " realising the security " is only possible by making the debtor a slave, and as this is very painful, the creditor who makes much use of it is hated. Even when the land can be pledged, peasant proprietors never think that it ought really to be taken if the debt for which it is pledged is not paid. They think that the land is still theirs, no matter how much has been lent them upon it, or how much they have neglected to pay. But odious as the " usurer " thus becomes, he is most useful really, and the beginner of the movement which creates the " great commerce ".

Another condition which precedes the free transfer of labour—the first prerequisite of the free transfer of capital—is slavery, and within its limits this is free enough ; indeed, more free than anything else

similar, for you have not to consult the labourer at
all, as in all other organisations you must. The
capitalist buys the slave and sets him to do, not
what the slave likes, but what he himself likes. I
can imagine that a theorist would say beforehand
that this was the best way of getting things done,
though not for the happiness of the doer. It makes
the "working group" into an army where the
general is absolute, and desertion penal. But so
subtle is the nature of things, that actual trial shows
this structure of society not to be industrially
superior to all others, but to be very ineffectual
indeed, and industrially inferior to most of them.
The slave will not work except he is made, and
therefore he does little; he is none the better, or
little the better, if he does his work well than if he
does it ill, and therefore he rarely cares to do it very
well. On a small scale, and under careful super-
vision, a few slaves carefully trained may be made
to do very good work, but on any large scale it is
impossible. A gang of slaves can do nothing but
what is most simple and easy, and most capable of
being looked after. The Southern States of America,
for some years before their rebellion, were engaged
in trying on the greatest scale and with the most
ample means the world has ever seen the experiment
how far slavery would go; and the result is easily
stated; they never could "make brute force go
beyond brute work".

Next, in order that capital can be transferred,
it must exist and be at the disposal of persons
who wish to transfer it. This is especially evident

as to remunerative capital, which we have seen
to be the most transferable of all capital. But the
earliest wages-paying commodities—the food and
the necessaries which in simple communities the
labourer desires—are accumulated by persons who
want them for their own use, and who will not part
with them. The "untransferable" labourer—the
labourer confined to a single occupation in a primitive
society—saves certain things for himself, and needs
them for himself, but he has no extra stock. He
has no use, indeed, for it. In a society where there
is no transferable labour, or need to hire, there is
no motive, or almost none, for an accumulation
of wages-paying capital which is to buy labour.
The idea of it, simple as it seems to us, is one
of a much later age, like that in which labour
seeking to be hired is the commonest of things,
and therefore the commodities needed for hiring it
are among the commonest too. The means of buying, and the thing bought, inevitably in such a
case as this grow together.

As to the other kind of capital—that which aids
labour, the co-operative kind—the scientific study
of savage tribes, which is so peculiar a feature of
the present world, has brought out its scantiness—
I might say its meanness—almost more distinctly
than it has brought out anything else. Sir John
Lubbock, one of our greatest instructors on this
matter, tells us the implements of the Australians
are very simple. "They have no knowledge of
pottery, and carry water in skins, or in vessels made
of bark. They are quite ignorant of warm water,

which strikes them with great amazement." Some
of them carry "a small bag about the size of a
moderate cabbage net, which is made by laying
threads, loop within loop, somewhat in the manner
of knitting used by our ladies to make purses. This
bag the man carries loose upon his back by a small
string, which passes over his head ; it generally contains a lump or two of paint and resin, some fish-
hooks and lines, a shell or two out of which these
hooks are made, a few points of darts, and their
usual ornaments, which include the whole worldly
treasure of the richest man among them."   All
travellers say that rude nations have no *stock* of anything—no materials lying ready to be worked up,
no idle tools waiting to be used ; the whole is a
" hand-to-mouth " world.   And this is but another
way of saying that in such societies there is no
capital of this kind to be transferred.   We said just
now that what we meant by transfer in such a case
was a change in the sort of stock—the kind of
materials, the kind of machines, the kind of living
things to be used fastest and worn out quickest.
But in these poverty-stricken early societies there is
substantially no such stock at all.   Every petty thing
which there exists is already being used for all its
petty purposes, and cannot be worked more quickly
than it already is, or be worn out more rapidly than
it is being worn out.

Next, this capital must be concentrated in "trades,"
else it cannot be transferred from trade to trade for
the sake of profit, and it must be worked by a single
capitalist, or little group of capitalists, as the case

may be, else the trade will not yield profit. And this, as has been explained, is not a universal feature of all times, but a special characteristic of somewhat advanced eras. And there must be the knowledge capable of employing that capital—a knowledge which altogether differs in different trades. Now-a-days the amount of the difference is a little disguised from us because we see people with "capital" in various pursuits—that is, who are traders in each and all of them. But such persons could not do this unless they were assisted by more specialised persons. The same principle governs political administration. Sir George Lewis, one of the most capable judges of it in our time, has observed: "The permanent officers of a department are the depositaries of its official tradition ; they are generally referred to by the political head of the office for information on questions of official practice, and knowledge of this sort acquired in one department would be useless in another. If, for example, the chief clerk of the criminal department of the Home Office were to be transferred to the Foreign Office, or to the Admiralty, the special experience which he has acquired at the Home Office, and which is in daily requisition for the guidance of the Home Secretary, would be utterly valueless to the Foreign Secretary, or to the First Lord of the Admiralty. . . . Where a general superintendence is required, and assistance can be obtained from subordinates, and where the chief qualifications are judgment, sagacity, and enlightened political opinions, such a change of offices is possible; but as you descend lower in the official scale, the speciality of functions increases. The duties must be performed in person, with little or no assistance, and there is consequently a necessity for special knowledge and experience. Hence the same person may be successively at the head of the Home Office, the Foreign Office, the Colonial Office and the Admiralty; he may be successively President of the Board of Trade, and Chancellor of the Exchequer; but to transfer an experienced clerk from one office to another would be like transferring a skilful naval officer to the army, or appointing a military engineer officer to command a ship of war." And just so in mercantile business—there are certain general principles which are common to all kinds of it, and a person can be of considerable use in more than one kind if he understands these principles, and has the proper sort of mind. But the appearance of this common element is in commerce, as in politics, a sign of magnitude, and primitive commerce is all petty. In early tribes there is nothing but the special man—the clothier, the mason, the weapon-maker. Each craft tried to be, and very much was, a mystery except to those who carried it on. The knowledge required for each was possessed by few, kept secret by those few, and nothing else was of use but this monopolised and often inherited acquirement; there was no "general" business knowledge. The idea of a general art of money-making is very modern; almost everything ancient about it is individual and particular. Distance helped much in this kind of speciality. "To the great fair of Stourbridge," in the south of England, there came, we are told, besides foreign products, "the woolpacks, which then formed the riches of England, and were the envy of outer nations. The Cornish tin-mine sent its produce, stamped with the sign of the rich earl who bought the throne of the German empire, or of the warlike prince who had won his spurs at Crécy, and captured the French king at Poitiers. . . . Thither came also salt from the springs of Worcestershire, as well as that which had been gathered under the summer sun from the salterns of the eastern coasts. Here, too, might be found lead from the mines of Derbyshire, and iron, either raw or manufactured, from the Sussex forges."[1] In an age when locomotion was tedious and costly, the mere distance of the separate seats of industry tended to make separate monopolies of them. Other difficulties of transferring capital were aggravated by the rarity and the localisation of the knowledge necessary for carrying it on.

Next, as we have seen, for the attraction of capital from trade to trade, there must be a money in which to calculate such profits, and a good money too. Many media of interchange which have been widely used in the world, and which are quite good enough for many purposes, are quite unfit for this. Cattle, for instance, which were certainly one of the first-used kinds of money, and which have been said to have been that most used, because what we call the primitive ages lasted so long, are quite inadequate.

[1] Thorold Rogers.

They are good enough for present bargains, but not for the forward- and backward-looking calculations of profit and loss. The notation is not distinct enough for accuracy. One cow is not exactly like another; a price-list saying that so much raw cotton was worth twenty cows, and so much cotton worth thirty cows, would not tell much for the purpose; you could not be sure what cows you would have to give or you would get. There might be a "loss by exchange" which would annihilate profit. Until you get good coined money, calculations of profit and loss that could guide capital are impossible.

Next, there must be the means of shifting "money," which we analysed—the loan fund, the speculative fund, and the choice of employment by young capitalists, or some of them. The loan fund on a small scale is, as we have seen, a very early institution; it begins in the primitive village almost as soon as any kind of trade begins at all, and a perception of its enormous value is one of the earliest pieces of true economic speculation. "In the Athenian laws," says Demosthenes, "are many well-devised securities for the protection of the creditor; for commerce proceeds not from the borrowers, but from the lenders, without whom no vessel, no navigator, no traveller could depart from port." Even in these days we could hardly put the value of discounts and trade loans higher. But though the loan fund begins so early in civilisation, and is prized so soon, it grows very slowly; the full development, modern banking such as we are familiar with in England, stops where the English language ceases to be spoken. The peculiarity of that system is that it utilises all the petty cash of private persons down nearly to the end of the middle class. This is lodged with bankers on running account, and though incessantly changing in distribution, the quantity is nearly fixed on the whole, for most of what one person pays out others almost directly pay in; and therefore it is so much added to the loan fund which bankers have to use, though, as credit is always precarious, they can, of course, only use it with caution. Besides this, English bankers have most of the permanent savings of little persons deposited with them, and so have an unexampled power of ready lending. But ages of diffused confidence are necessary to establish such a system, and peculiar circumstances in the banking history of England, and of Scotland still more, have favoured it. Our insular position exempting us from war, and enabling our free institutions to develop both quietly and effectually, is at the very root of it. But here until within a hundred years there was no such concentration of minute moneys, no such increment to the loan fund, and abroad there is nothing equal to it now. Taking history as a whole, it is a rare and special phenomenon. Mostly the loan fund of a country consists of such parts of its moneyed savings as those who have saved them are able to lend for themselves. As countries advance banking slowly begins, and some persons who are believed to have much, are intrusted with the money of others, and become a sort of middlemen to put it out; but almost everywhere the loan fund is very small to our English notions. It is a far less efficient instrument for conveying capital from trade to trade everywhere else than here; in very many countries it is only incipient; in some it can hardly be said to exist at all.

The speculative fund, as I have called it, has also but a bounded range of action. The number of persons who have large moneyed savings who are willing to invest them in new things is in England considerable, but in most countries it is small. Such persons fear the unknown; they have a good deal to lose, and they do not wish to lose it. In most communities there is not even the beginning of a settled opinion to tell them which undertaking is likely to be good, and which bad. In the industrial history of most countries, the most marked feature is an extreme monotony; enterprises are few; the same things continue for ages to be done in the same way. The *data* which should guide original minds are few and insufficient; there was not such a thing as a " price list " in any ancient community. No Athenian merchant could, by looking over a file of figures, see which commodities were much lower in their average price, and which therefore might be advantageously bought with money that he could not employ in his usual trade. Even for so simple a speculation as this, according to our present notions, the *data* did not exist, and for more complex ones the knowledge was either altogether wanting or confined to a few persons, none of whom might have the idle capital. The speculative fund does not become a force of first-rate magnitude till we have in the same community a great accumulation of spare capital, and a wide diffusion of sound trade knowledge,—and then it does.

The free choice by young men of the mode in which they will invest the capital which they possess, is also in the early times of trade much hindered and cramped, and it only gains anything near the effective influence which it now has with us, in quite late times. For a long period of industrial history special associations called "guilds" prohibited it; these kept each trade apart, and prevented capital from going from one to the other. They even kept the trade of city A quite apart from the same trade in city B; they would not let capital or labour flow from one to the other. These restrictive hedges grew up naturally, and there was no great movement to throw them down. They strengthened what was already strong, and that which was weak made no protest. The general ignorance of trade matters in such communities made it seem quite reasonable to keep each trade to those who understood it; other people going into it would, it was imagined, only do it ill, lose their money, and hurt those who did it well by a pernicious competition. We now know that this is a great error, that such guilds did far more harm than good, that only experiment can show where capital will answer in trade, that it is from the outsider that the best improvements commonly come. But these things, which are now commonplaces after experience, were paradoxes before it. The first deduction of the uninstructed mind was and is the other way. Nor is it dispelled by mere argument. Civilisation must increase, trade ideas must grow and spread, and idle capital waiting to change must accumulate. Till these things have happened, the free choice by a young man how he will invest his capital is not the common rule, but the rare exception; it is not what mostly happens, though it may be resisted, but what happens only where it is unusually helped. Even where there is no formal guild, the circumstances which have elsewhere created so many, create an informal monopoly, mostly much stronger than any force which strives to infringe it.

None, therefore, of the three instruments which now convey capital from employment to employment can in early times be relied on for doing so, even when that capital exists, and when some labour at least is available to be employed by it; neither the loan fund, nor the speculative fund, nor the free choice of a trade by young men, is then a commonly predominant power; nor do the whole three taken together commonly come to much in comparison with the forces opposed to them.

And even if their intrinsic strength had been far greater than it was, it would often have been successfully impeded by the want of a final condition to the free transfer of capital, of which I have not spoken yet. This is a political condition. We have seen that for the free transfer of labour from employment to employment a strong government is necessary. The rules regulating the inheritance of trades and the fixed separations of labour were really contrivances to obtain some part of the results of the division of labour, when for want of an effectual government, punishing quarrels and preserving life, free competition and movement in labour were impossible. And this same effectual government is equally necessary, as need not be explained, for the free migration of money. That migration needs peace and order quite as obviously as the migration of labour; and those who understand the delicacy of the process will need no proof of it. But though a strong government is required, something more is wanted too; for the movement of capital we need a *fair* government. If capital is to be tempted from trade to trade by the prospect of high profits, it must be allowed to keep those profits when they have been made. But the primitive notion of taxation is that when a government sees much money it should take some of it, and that if it sees more money it should take more of it. Adam Smith laid down, as a fundamental canon, that taxes ought to be levied at the time when, and in the manner in which, it is most easy for the tax-payer to pay them. But the primitive rule is to take them when and how it is most easy to find and seize them. Under governments with that rule persons who are doing well shrink from showing that they are doing well; those who are making money refuse to enjoy themselves, and will show none of the natural signs of that money, lest the tax-gatherer should appear and should take as much as he likes of it. A socialist speaker once spoke of a "*healthy* habit of confiscation," and that habit has been much diffused over the world. Wherever it exists it is sure exceedingly to impede the movements of capital, and where it abounds to prevent them.

These reasonings give us a conception of a " pre-economic " era when the fundamental postulates of Political Economy, of which we have spoken, were not realised, and show us that the beginnings of all wealth were made in that era. Primitive capital accumulated in the hands of men who could neither move it nor themselves—who really never thought of doing either—to whom either would often have seemed monstrous if they could have thought of it, and in whose case either was still more often prevented by insuperable difficulties. And this should warn us not to trust the historical retrospect of economists, merely because we see and know that their reasonings on the events and causes of the present world are right. Early times had different events and different causes. Reasoners like economists, and there are many others like them, are apt to modify the famous saying of Plunket; they turn history not into an old almanac, but into a new one. They make what happens now to have happened always, according to the same course of time.

And these reasonings also enable us to explain what is so common in all writing concerning those early and pre-economic times. One of the commonest phenomena of primitive trade is " fixed " prices, and the natural inquiry of every one who is trained in our Political Economy is, how could these prices be maintained? They seem impossible according to the teaching which he has received, and yet they were maintained for ages; they lasted longer than many things now-a-days which we do not reckon short-lived. One explanation is that they were maintained by custom ; but this fails at the crisis, for the question is, how could the custom be maintained ? The unchanging price could not always be right under changing circumstances. Why did not capital and labour flow into the trades which at the time had more than their "natural" price, desert those which had less, and so disturb the first with a plethora, and the second with a scarcity? The answer we now see is that what we have been used to call "natural" is not the first but the second nature of men ; that there were ages when capital and labour could not migrate, when trade was very much one of monopoly against monopoly. And in such a society, fixing a price is a primitive way of doing what in after ages we do as far as we can ; it is a mode of regulating the monopoly—of preventing the incessant dissensions which in all ages arise about what is a just price and what is not, when there is no competition to settle that price. The way in which "custom" settles prices, how it gradually arrives at what is right and proper, or at least at what is endurable, one cannot well say ; probably many incipient customary prices break down before the one which suits and lasts is stumbled upon. But defects of this rule-of-thumb method are no reproach to primitive times. When we try to regulate monopolies ourselves we have arrived at nothing better. The fares of railways—the fixed prices at which these great monopolies carry passengers—are as accidental, as much the rough results of inconclusive experiments, as any prices can be.

And this long analysis proves so plainly, that it

would be tedious to show it again, that the free movement of capital from employment to employment within a nation, and the consequent strong tendency to an equality of profits there, are ideals daily becoming truer as competition increases and capital grows, that all the hindrances are gradually diminishing, all the incentives enhancing, and all the instruments becoming keener, quicker, and more powerful.

But it is most important to observe that this ideal of English Political Economy is not, like most of its ideals, an ultimate one. In fact the "great commerce" has already gone beyond it; we can already distinctly foresee a time when that commerce will have merged it in something larger. English Political Economy, as we know, says that capital fluctuates from trade to trade within a nation, and it adds that capital will not as a rule migrate beyond that nation. "Feelings," says Ricardo, "which I should be sorry to see weakened, induced most men of property to be satisfied with a low rate of profits in their own country, rather than seek a more advantageous employment for their wealth in foreign nations." But these feelings are being weakened every day. A class of cosmopolitan capitalists has grown up which scarcely feels them at all. When Ricardo wrote, trade of the modern magnitude was new: long wars had separated most nations from most others, and especially had isolated England in habit and in feeling. Ricardo framed, and others have continued, a theory of foreign trade in which each nation is bounded by a ring-fence, through which capital cannot pass in or out. But the present state of things is far less simple, and much of that theory must be remodelled. The truth is that the three great instruments for transferring capital within a nation, whose operation we have analysed, have begun to operate on the largest scale between nations. The "loan fund," the first and most powerful of these, does so most strikingly. Whenever the English money market is bare of cash it can at once obtain it by raising the rate of interest. That is to say, it can borrow money to the extent of millions at any moment to meet its occasions: or what is the same thing, can call in loans of its own. Other nations can do so too, each in proportion to its credit and its wealth—though none so quickly as England, on account of our superiority in these things. A cosmopolitan loan fund exists, which runs everywhere as it is wanted, and as the rate of interest tempts it.

A new commodity, one of the greatest growths of recent times, is used to aid these operations. The "securities" of all well-known countries, their national debts, their railway shares, and so on (a kind of properties peculiar to the last two centuries, and increasing now most rapidly), are dealt in through Europe on every Stock Exchange. If the rate of interest rises in any one country the price of such securities falls; foreign countries come in and buy them; they are sent abroad and their purchase-money comes here. Such interest-bearing documents are a sort of national "notes of hand" which a country puts out when it is poor, and buys back when it is rich.

The mode in which the indemnity from France to Germany was paid is the most striking instance of this which ever occurred in the world. The sum of £200,000,000 was the largest ever paid by one set of persons to another, upon a single contract, since the system of payments began. Without a great lending apparatus such an operation could not have been effected. The resources of one nation, as nations now are, would not have been equal to it. In fact it was the international loan fund which did the business. "We may say," M. Say states in his official report, "that all the great banking-houses of Europe have concurred in this operation, and it is sufficient to show the extent and the magnitude of it to say that the number of houses which signed or concurred in the arrangement was fifty-five, and that many of them represented syndicates of bankers, so that the actual number concerned was far more considerable." "The concentration," he adds, "of the effects of all the banks of Europe produced results of an unhoped-for magnitude. All other business of a similar nature was almost suspended for a time, while the capital of all the private banks, and of all their friends, co-operated in the success of the French loans, and in the transmission of the money lent from country to country. This was a new fact in the economic history of Europe, and we should attach peculiar importance to it." The magnitude of it as a single transaction was indeed very new; but it is only a magnificent instance of what incessantly happens; and the commonness of similar small transactions, and the amount of

them when added together, are even more remarkable and even more important than the size of this
one ; and similar operations of the international
"loan fund" are going on constantly, though on
a far less scale.

We must not, however, fancy that this puts all
countries on a level, as far as capital is concerned,
because it can be attracted from one to another.
On the contrary, there will always tend to be a fixed
difference between two kinds of countries. The old
country, where capital accumulates, will always, on
an average, have it cheaper than the new country,
which has saved little, and can employ any quantity.
The Americans in the Mississippi Valley are naturally
a borrowing community, and the English at home
are naturally lenders. And the rate of interest in
the lending country will of course be less than that
in the borrowing country. We see approaches—
distant approaches even yet, but still distinct approaches—to a time at which all civilised and industrial countries will be able to obtain a propor-
tionate share of the international loan fund, and will
differ only in the rate they have to pay for it.

The "speculative fund" is also becoming common
to all countries, and it is the English who have
taken the lead, because they have more money, more
practical adaptation to circumstances, and more industrial courage than other nations. Some nations,
no doubt, have as much or more of one of these
singly, but none have as much of the efficiency which
is the combined result of all three. The way in which
continental railways—the early ones especially, when

the idea was novel—were made by English con-
tractors is an example of this. When Mr. Brassey,
the greatest of them, was making the line from Turin
to Novara, for the Italian Government, Count
Cavour sent one morning for his agent, and said:
"We are in a difficulty: the public have subscribed
for very few shares, but I am determined to carry
out the line, and I want to know if Mr. Brassey will
take half the deficiency if the Italian Government
will take the other half". Mr. Brassey did so, and
thus the railway was made. This is the international speculative fund in action, and the world
is filled with its triumphs.

So large, so daring, and indeed often so reckless
is this speculative fund, that some persons have
imagined that there was nothing which would seem
absurd to it. A very little while ago, a scheme—a
fraudulent scheme, no doubt—was gravely brought
out, for a ship railway over the Isthmus of Panama;
the ships were to be lifted upon the line on one side,
and lifted off and returned to the ocean on the other.
But even the "speculative fund" would not stand
that, and the scheme collapsed. Yet the caricature
shows the reality; we may use it to remind ourselves
how mobile this sort of money is, and how it runs
from country to country like beads of quicksilver.

Young men also now transfer their capital from
country to country with a rapidity formerly unknown.
In Europe perhaps the Germans are most eminent
in so doing. Their better school education, their
better-trained habits of learning modern languages,
and their readiness to bear the many privations of

a residence among foreigners, have gained them a prominence certainly over the English and the French, perhaps above all other nations. But taking the world as a whole the English have a vast superiority. They have more capital to transfer, and their language is the language of the great commerce everywhere, and tends to become so more and more. More transactions of the "cosmopolitan speculative fund" are arranged in English, probably, than in all the other languages of the world put together; not only because of the wealth and influence of mere England, though that is not small, but because of the wealth and influence of the other States which speak that language also, the United States, our colonies, and British India, which uses it mostly for its largest trade. The number of English commercial houses all over the world is immense, and of American very many, and yearly a vast number of young Englishmen are sent out to join them. The pay is high, the prospect good, and insular as we are thought to be (and in some respects we are so most mischievously), the emigration of young men with English capital, and to manage English capital, is one of the great instruments of world-wide trade and one of the binding forces of the future.

In this way the same instruments which diffused capital through a nation are gradually diffusing it among nations. And the effect of this will be in the end much to simplify the problems of international trade. But for the present, as is commonly the case with incipient causes whose effect is incomplete, it complicates all it touches. We still have to consider, after the manner Ricardo began, international trade as one between two or more limits which do not interchange their compound capitals, and then to consider how much the conclusions so drawn are modified by new circumstances and new causes. And as even when conceived in Ricardo's comparatively simple manner, international trade, as Mr. Mill justly said, and as the readers of his discussion on it well know, is an excessively difficult subject of inquiry, we may expect to find many parts of it very hard indeed to reduce to anything like simplicity when new encumbrances are added. The popular discussion of the subject tends to conceal its difficulties, and indeed is mostly conducted by those who do not see them. Nothing is commoner than to see statements on it put forth as axioms which it would take half a book really to prove or disprove. But with the soundness or unsoundness of such arguments I have at present nothing to do. The object of these papers is not to examine the edifice of our English Political Economy, but to define its basis. Nothing but unreality can come of it till we know when and how far its first assertions are true in matter of fact, and when and how far they are not.

THE PRELIMINARIES

OF

POLITICAL ECONOMY.[1]

Adam Smith began the *Wealth of Nations* about 1773, and finished it in 1776; and as our modern Political Economy really begins from that time, we may fairly say that it is now a hundred years old.[2] In that century, especially in England, its career has been most remarkable. No form of philosophical speculation (some theologies excepted, which are not comparable) has ever had half or a thousandth part of the influence upon life and practice; no abstract doctrine was ever half as much quoted or half as much acted on. The whole legislation of England as to trade has been changed by the philosophy of trade, and the life of almost every one in England is, in consequence, different and better. Other countries, it is true, have not equally followed

---

[1] It will be obvious that some of the leading ideas of the previous essays are repeated in this. There is, however, so much that is fresh in it, and so much danger of bungling in any attempt to disentangle the fresh matter from what was embodied in the two previous essays, that it has been thought better to run some little risk of repetition rather than to attempt any separation of the old and new by any other hand than the author's.

[2] Written in 1876 or earlier.

this teaching, but they have continually, if not equally, discussed it. The highest class of culti-vated intellects is in every civilised country more or less affected by it. When a little while ago M. Thiers began to talk and act in thorough opposition to the whole science, a shiver of wonder ran through Europe; it seemed an anachronism to find so able a mind in the pre-economic period, and a strange survival of extinct error, to hear him expounding the good of all which Political Economy showed to be bad, and the evil of all which Political Economy proved to be good. No kind of political teaching has ever won half as many triumphs, or produced half the effects.

But, nevertheless, the reputation of Political Economy is not altogether satisfactory to the minds of those who most value and prize it. There is not quite the same interest felt for it, or quite the same confidence reposed in it, which there was formerly. A small knot of persons deny its value; a good many people, though sure they are wrong, are puzzled by them, and do not see how to answer them. Many young men, even studious men, especially those educated abroad, have not studied its best writers, and have but vague views about it. Though vic-torious, it wants part of the prestige of victory; though rich in results, its credit is not quite as good as on that account it ought to be.

The truth is that the story of Political Economy, if I may so call it, is a curious one in itself; the science is to some extent a new sort of one in the world, and has come to be what it is in a rather strange way. That story could only be fully explained by an exposition of all the science, and an account of all who contributed to it. But I think the main and most valuable part of the truth may be set before those who will read a short description of the science as it now stands, and a rough account of the labours of four great men, [1] who more than any others, have made the science what it is, and placed it where it is. The knowledge so given will after all be most imperfect.

Political Economy in its complete form, and as we now have it, is an abstract science, just as statics or dynamics are deductive sciences. And, in consequence, it deals with an unreal and imaginary subject. Just as statics and dynamics—the sciences of theoretical mechanics—deal with perfectly rigid bodies, which nothing will bend or strain; with perfectly elastic planes, from which the rebound is equal to the impact ; with a world destitute of friction ; with physical materials in short which no one ever expects to find in reality—so Political Economy deals with an immaterial subject, which in the existing world cannot be found either. Political Economy deals not with the entire real man as we know him in fact, but with a simpler, imaginary man—a man answering to a pure definition from which all impairing and conflicting elements have been fined away. The abstract man of this science is engrossed with one desire only—the desire of possessing wealth, not of course that there ever was a

[1] The essay on J. S. Mill was not written and that on Adam Smith is incomplete.

being who always acted as that desire would dictate, any more than any one thinks there is in nature a world without friction or entirely elastic planes, but because it is found convenient to isolate the effects of this force from all others. The effect of the abstract hypothesis, made on the necessary basis of statics and dynamics, is to enable us to see the effect of the single agent, "pressure," in a simple way and free from the repressing and obscuring conditions which exist in actual nature. And in the same way the use of the primitive assumptions of Political Economy is to show how the greatest of industrial desires—the desire to obtain wealth—would operate, if we consider it as operating, as far as we possibly can, by itself. The maxim of science is simply that of common-sense—simple cases first; begin with seeing how the main force acts when there is as little as possible to impede it, and when you thoroughly comprehend that, add to it in succession the separate effects of each of the encumbering and interfering agencies.

If such a simplification is necessary in physical science where the forces are obvious and few, it must much more be necessary in dealing with the science of society, where the forces are, in comparison, very various and difficult to perceive. In this very science of Political Economy, the first writers endeavoured to deal in a single science with all the causes which produced or impaired wealth—which, as they would have said, "made nations rich or poor". And this was the most natural way of beginning. Almost all science seems to have begun similarly. In each

case there was some large palpable fact to be explained—some great pressing problem to be solved.
And so here, if you look over the nations of the
world, you see at once that one of the greatest contrasts between them is that of comparative wealth,
or comparative poverty ; the palpable fact at the
beginning of Political Economy is that the Dutch
are rich, and others (the Tyrolese, suppose), poor—
that England is a very rich country, and Ireland a
very poor country ; how then was this difference to
be accounted for, and the practical problem—money
being an admitted good—to be solved, how far can
we make the poor nations rich, and how are we to
begin so to do ?   But considered in this simple and
practical way, the science of Political Economy becomes useless, because of its immense extent.   The
whole of a man's nature, and the whole of his circumstances, must be reckoned up and reasoned upon
before you can explain his comparative wealth or
poverty.   To explain the difference of industrial
conditions between the Tyrol and Holland, you will
have, first, to state all the points of difference in
religion, in morality, and in inherited character between a Dutchman and a Tyrolese—then state the
diversities of their physical condition, and work out,
as best you can, the effects of all the contrasts.   And
still further, if you try to give a universal reason why
nations are poor and why nations are rich, you will
not be able to arrive at any useful answer.   Some
will be poor because they have a bad government ;
some because they are cooped up on a poor soil ;
some because they have a religion which disinclines

them to make money; some because they have
ancient rules, which helped them to make a beginning, but now retard them; some because they have
never been able to make that beginning; and many
other causes might be given. The problem taken up
in that form is indeterminate; why nations are rich
or poor depends on the whole intrinsic nature, and
all the outward circumstances, of such nations.
There is no simpler formula to be discovered, and a
science which attempted to find one would of necessity have to deal with the whole of physical science;
it would be an account of all "men" and all the
earth.

It is on account of its abstract character that
Political Economy is often, and justly described, as
a science of "tendencies" only; that is, the object
of it is to work out and ascertain the result of certain
great forces, as if these alone operated, and as if
nothing else had any effect in the matter. But as
in matter of fact many other forces have an effect,
the computed results of the larger isolated forces
will never exactly happen; they will only, as it is
said, tend more or less to happen; that is, they
happen more and more nearly in proportion as the
resisting and perturbing causes in each case happen
to be less and less.

The very refined nature of the modern science of
Political Economy has naturally led to many mistakes about it. The mere idea of such a science has
evidently never crossed the minds of many able
writers, and persons who have given but slight consideration to the matter are much puzzled. Analo-

gous sciences of physical subjects are, as has been said, easy to find, but illustrations from them do not tell much where effectual description of Political Economy is most wanted. A science occupied with human things, and professedly with a part of human things profoundly interesting, awakens a great curiosity among multitudes of little cultivation. They begin to think about it, and to read about it, and the better the books they read, the more likely are they to be puzzled by what they find. They know that they are reading words which are constantly used in common life, and about things resembling, at least, those of that life, but nevertheless the reasonings and the conclusions do not seem to belong to real life at all. Such persons know nothing about statics or dynamics ; and any attempt to explain the nature of Political Economy by an account of the nature of statics or dynamics, is only explaining *obscurum per obscurius.* As might be expected, the worst offenders are the uncultured moralists. They see all manner of reasonings framed, and of conclusions drawn, apparently about subjects with which morality itself is concerned deeply—about (say) industry and wealth, population and poverty, and they never dream that there is anything peculiar about these conclusions. They apply the "rules of morality" to them at once; they ask: "Is argument B true of good persons ? Would not conclusion C augment wickedness?" whereas, in fact, the economic writers under consideration did not mean (and rightly did not mean) to deal with ethics at all. They only evolved a hypothesis; they did not intend that their arguments should be thought to be taken from real life, or that their conclusions should be roughly, and as they stood, applied to real life. They considered not the whole of actual human nature, but only a part of it. They dealt not with man, the moral being, but with man, the money-making animal.

Naturally, too, the cultivators of the abstract science itself (even those who fully understood its peculiar nature), did not always in practice remember the remoteness to practice of that nature. On the contrary, they rushed forth into the world with hasty recommendations to instant action ; whereas the very justification of their reasonings, and the very ground of their axioms, was the necessity of beginning the investigation of the subject in a simple theory, and far away from the complexities of practice and action. But so much are the practical impulses of man stronger than his theoretical tastes, that the cultivators of an abstract science are always in great danger of forgetting its abstract nature; they rush and act on it at once. In the abstract physical sciences there is an effectual penalty. A person who acted on abstract dynamics would soon break his head, but in mental and physical sciences unhappily there are no instant tests of failure. Whatever happens, a man can always argue that he was right ; and thus an abstract science of human things is more delicate to handle, and more likely to be misused, than a similar science of external nature.

A sort of uncertainty likewise seems, even in the better-informed minds, to creep over the subject. If it is so remote from practice, they say, how can you test it, and how can you tell that it is true ? But this is exactly so also in the corresponding physical sciences. One of the shrewdest observers of intellectual matters of the generation, the late Sir G. C. Lewis, used to say : " My experience in this office " (he was then Secretary of State for War) " has convinced me that when you come to practice, physics are just as uncertain as metaphysics. The abstract theory of physics is unquestionably much more complete, but if you want to deal with an instance in life, you will always find that there is a ' tension,' or a ' friction,' or some other cause, which is not accurately measured, and does not figure in the abstract theory. And this is the reason why, on all such questions, scientific evidence is so conflicting. You can always obtain an eminent engineer on any side to set against an eminent engineer on the other side, because the scientific and certain part of the subject is not the whole, and there still remains an imperfectly explored *residuum* on which there may be different opinions." All this is as true of Political Economy as of any physical science ; its deductions may be incontrovertible, and its results precisely true, whenever its assumptions are true, but these results will be very imperfect guides, wherever those assumptions are impaired by contradictory matter.

On the other side, however, it should also be said that " abstract " Political Economy is not by any means the unnatural thing which, from the account of it on paper, and the description of its difficulties, it would seem to be. Many people on the matter have " talked prose all their lives without knowing

it "; many people have given admirable arguments
on Political Economy, and have been more or less
precisely aware of the difference of their assumptions
from those of the real world, though they have never
studied the specially abstract science, and could
have given no sufficient delineation of it.   The notion
of investigating how much money persons would
make, who simply wished to make it, and how they
would best do so, is a very simple idea.   The desire
for wealth—using wealth in the largest sense, so as
to include not only the means of luxury, but the
means of subsistence—is so preponderant in very
many minds, that it is very easy, if necessary,
to regard it as the sole object.   As far as people are
what we now always call men of business, money,
the thing they look for and the thing they want, is
their sole object, and in that sense of the phrase,
Political Economy may be fairly called the science
of " business ".

On that account, in some very large scenes of our
present English life, Political Economy is exactly
true.   The primary assumption on which it rests
is precisely realised.   On the Stock Exchange everybody does act from a love of money ; men come
there to make it, and they try to make as much of it
as they can.   Of Lombard Street the same may be
said ; the pecuniary phenomena of Lombard Street
may be investigated with quite sufficient accuracy,
on the assumption that bankers come there only
to make money, and when there, make as much of it
as they can.   All markets are scenes nearly similar ;
so long as they are at the market all dealers try to

make the best bargain they can. As the principal
nations of the world at present are nations of business
—commercial nations—and as the mass of men in
such nations are mainly occupied in business, it
follows that with respect to those nations a simple
analysis of the unchecked consequences of the
" business motive" will be a near approximation
to a large part of their life, though it will not be a
perfect account of their complete career, for there is
very much also in every nation besides business
and besides money—but it will be a useful hint to a
predominant characteristic of that career. Having
investigated the effects of this principal motive, we
may when we please, and as far as it is necessary,
investigate the effects of the almost infinite number
of the secondary and interfering motives.

As, too, it is at present necessary for all nations
to be rich in order to be influential in the world, it
follows further, that an account of the commercial
motive of action, taken by itself, is, as the world now
stands, an analysis of the results of a principal
ingredient in the days that are gone by, when poor
barbarians, if warlike, were more powerful than rich
civilised people. The times are gone by when
civilisation enervated energy, or when wealth impeded valour. At present, courage without money
is courage without guns ; and courage without guns
is useless. Political Economy traces, in an abstract
way, the effects of the desire to be rich, and nations
must now-a-days abound in that passion if they are
to have much power or much respect in the world.

On the other hand, no intellectual attempt can be

more absurd than the attempt to apply the conclusions of our Political Economy to the lives of
nations at a non-commercial stage of their existence.
A great military nation, based on slavery, like the
Romans; a nation bound by fixed customs like so
many Oriental nations; tribes in a state of barbarism,—are not guided principally by the commercial
spirit.   The money-getting element is a most subordinate one in their minds; its effects are very
subordinate ones in their lives.   As the commercial
element is all but necessary to considerable combinations of men, that element will almost always
have effects, and usually important effects, in the
destiny of these combinations.   But only in communities where the commercial element is the
greatest element, will these effects be the greatest.
In so far as nations are occupied in " buying and
selling," in so far will Political Economy, the exclusive theory of men buying and selling, come out
right, and be true of them.

But it will be good as far as it goes, and, though
it is not my business to say it, I think it will be
the fault of the writer if the curious interest of the
facts does not lead many readers to a further study
of the subject.

And, though what has been explained is the
principal difference between the hypothetical science
of Political Economy and the real world, it is by
no means the only difference.   Just as this science
takes an abstract and one-sided view of man, who
is one of its subjects, so it also takes an abstract
and one-sided view of wealth, which is its other

subject. Wealth is infinitely various; as the wants
of human nature are almost innumerable, so the
kinds of wealth are various. Why men want so
many things is a great subject fit for inquiry.
Which of them it would be wise for men to want
more of, and which of them it would be wise to
want less of—are also great subjects equally fit.
But with these subjects Political Economy does not
deal at all; it leaves the first to the metaphysician,
who has to explain, if he can, the origin and the
order of human wants; and the second to the moral-
ist, who is to decide, to the best of his ability, which
of these tastes are to be encouraged, and when—
which to be discouraged, and when   The only
peculiarity of wealth with which the economist is
concerned is its *differentia specifica*—that which makes
it wealth. To do so it must gratify some want of
man, or it would not be desirable, or it would not
be wealth. But whence that want comes, whether
from a low part of man, or from a high, is to the
economist immaterial; whether it is a desirable want
for man to gratify he cares as little, so long as that
gratification does not hurt man as a wealth-produc-
ing machine. He regards a pot of beer and a
picture, a book of religion and a pack of cards, as
all equally " wealth," and therefore, for his purpose,
equally worthy of regard. The only division of
wealth in his mind is, if I may use the words, the
division between sterile and not sterile. Some
things will help men to make new things; some
things will induce men to work and make new
things; both these classes of things are in the eyes

of the economist capital or reproductive. On the
other hand, other things have no similar reproductive power; if they were taken out of the world all
work would go on with equal efficiency, and as
many new things would be produced. And these
last are, in the eyes of the economist, unproductive
opulence, just as the first were productive capital.

Further, Political Economy makes not only these
assumptions as to the nature of its principal force
and as to that of its object, it also makes two as to
the physical conditions under which this force acts,
and in which this object is supposed to exist. For
its own purposes it simplifies, as we have seen, the
nature of the actors, and the end of the action ;
we have now to see that it simplifies also the stage.

Political Economy assumes that land is " limited
in quantity and variable in quality ". And, taking
the whole of human states, this assumption has
almost always been true. There has been, in almost
all countries, a difficulty in obtaining land ; there
has scarcely ever been a surplus of it. Still, though
this assumption accurately coincides with the usual
phenomena of most countries, it does not agree with
all the phenomena of them all. On the contrary,
in all " new " countries, as they are called, land is
exceedingly plentiful. There is practically no difficulty in procuring it ; in the valley of the Mississippi
as much of the best land as any one wants can,
without serious impediment, be obtained. No doubt
such land is farther off from the best markets than
most occupied land of a like kind. But in the
present state of the arts such a difference in distance

presents no serious difficulty. The construction even of a short railway will open up an entire district, and make its produce as available in the market as that of much land long before cultivated. In new countries it can hardly be said that this assumption of Political Economy is at all the truth; it is rather the opposite of the truth. And accordingly the doctrines of abstract Political Economy must not be applied to such countries roughly, and without previous re-examination. One of the primitive assumptions not being true, we must be careful to reinvestigate and see whether any particular deduction which we wish to use, is, or is not, impaired —is, or is not, in consequence, untrue.

At first sight it would seem that this limitation of abstract Political Economy would exclude it from much of the real world. New countries, one would imagine, would be among the most common of countries; the human race has always been wandering, and must have been always reaching new countries. But, in truth, this limitation scarcely makes any new exclusion. The nature of the " man" who first occupied new countries did not " conform " to the standard of economic man; the being of reality was not the being of the hypothesis. The first men, all researches justify us in assuming, nearly approached in nature to the present savage man. They had not probably as many curious customs or so many debasing superstitions; they had not so many ingrained vices. But they had as little intellectual development, and as little knowledge of material things; they were ignorant of the " calen-

dar"; they could with difficulty count more than
five; they could just make a few weapons of war ;
they could just construct some sort of shed that
would serve for a dwelling; but they could not make
any of the articles which we now call "wealth";
and they would not have appreciated such things.
The desire, so strong in civilised man, for wealth, has
been excited in him by the experience of ages, and
has been transmitted to him by inheritance. If you
take a present savage, even of a high type, he will
find the life of cities, the life of wealth, *par excellence,*
scarcely tolerable. There is a well-known story of one
savage, who, after living some forty or fifty years in a
cultivated world, in his old age returned to die as a barbarian, saying "that civilisation was so much trouble
he could bear it no longer". The first occupiers of
most countries were not men eager for complex
wealth; they cared only for a bare subsistence—
and then to kill and eat one another.

Many ages, indeed, have always intervened between the first settlement of any country, and the
rise of a strong and independent mercantile element,
before the time at which the first assumption of
Political Economy was at all satisfied in it. During
that time such countries commenced a kind of
civilisation, but it was a very different kind of civilisation from the predominantly commercial; it was in
general ruled by fixed customs, as most of the East
is now; it did not allow its members to choose
their own ends and fix their own existence for themselves; on the contrary, it chose itself those ends
and prescribed that existence. And the life so

selected gave but little scope to the production of wealth. It was occupied either with an incessant military service, or, in peace, with an equally incessant but semi-religious ritual; the labour for, and the accumulation of, the means of physical comfort were very secondary aims in most of the periods described by history, as they still are in by far the greater part of the present world. For ages after their first colonisation, there was no such absorbing and self-selecting life of trade as Political Economy assumes and requires.

Accordingly, in all the old world—the world as known to the "ancients"—the land has long been occupied, and more or less usefully, more or less fully, by ancient and ineradicable races. In practice they cannot be dispossessed. In all that large part of the world, therefore, land is very scarce; no new comers can, in fact, obtain much of it. But of late there have been immense territories—"new worlds," to use the usual word—of which this is not true, but where the very reverse is true. Long voyages, impossible to the ancient navigator, have been made possible by modern inventions; and these voyages have discovered large regions inhabited only by men who fade away before the presence of civilised men. In these distant regions man seems to have been a protected, and, therefore, a feeble animal; he had not to submit to the incessant competition which has in the "old world" hardened his frame and seasoned his mind. The diseases which the European can bear, the stimulants in which he delights, the labour for which he lives, are so many poisons to the Australian or American savage. He dies of one or all of them soon after the coming of the European, and he leaves his land vacant. He has never been able to cultivate the land which he calls his, and now he drops away from it. As a singular result of this strange history, land of the best quality is now procurable in large quantities and with great ease by civilised man. There are now countries not only called "new," because newly discovered, but new, really, because the land in them can now be used, but has never been used before.

As a matter of fact, therefore, the primitive assumption of hypothetical Political Economy, that land is always limited in quantity, as well as variable in quality, coincides well enough with the usual facts of the world. But as the modern exception is one of great present importance to economic nations, as a matter of convenience it has become desirable (though I do not think the desirability has been usually recognised) to annex to Political Economy a full discussion of the nature and the effects of that exception. What has hitherto been the rule, and what has hitherto been the deviation from it, both become clearer when considered side by side.

It may be asked, what is the use of laying down such a rule, if you admit it, and discuss exceptions to it? Why invent a hypothetical hedge when you know that it does not include all you want, and that, therefore, you will be unable to keep within it? The answer is, that the rule was not arbitrarily invented by inward fancy, but suggested by outward facts long predominant. The nearest way to the whole truth is by pursuing the clue which the partial truth first gave.

Political Economy also assumes, as another axiomatic fact as to land, that land throughout the world is for the most part of such fertility that the labour of a cultivator, if he has but a very moderate degree of knowledge and skill, will produce not only a subsistence for himself, but also many other persons. This is so true that it perhaps scarcely needs to be said, but it is of cardinal importance. If it had not been true, the truths of Political Economy and the lives of men would have been altogether different from what they now are. And there is no *a priori* reason—in physics, at least—why the whole earth should not be as a bit of bleak moor, where agriculturists have nothing over, and can but just raise a bare subsistence for themselves. But for the most part there is a surplus, and this surplus is, of course, increased day by day. By the continual improvement in the arts of agriculture more is produced, and, therefore, there is more over. In old countries the increasing productiveness retards the need of a resort to new soils, and diminishes the evil of it; and in new countries this additional surplus is an extra fund for exportation, and a new means for supplying the wants of those who have stayed at home in the old world.

And, lastly, Political Economy declines to investigate all the causes which determine the rate of increase of man, and assumes an avowedly incomplete and approximate formula as to it. From the very nature of the case, Political Economy must do

this.   The causes which regulate the increase of
mankind are little less than all the causes outward
and inward which determine human action.   Climate,
social customs, political government, inherited race-
nature, and other things beside, affect, as we all
know, the rate at which population grows.   Political
Economy would have to discuss half physiology,
half the science of government, and half several
other sciences too, if it attempted to investigate the
real laws which regulate the multiplication of mankind ; it has necessarily to make an assumption, to
assume as a dictum some approximation to the
complex truth, which is at once simple enough to be
manageable, and true enough to be useful.   Political
Economy, therefore, assumes that in any particular
society the power of parents to produce children
exceeds the power to provide for them in what those
parents thinks sufficient comfort ; whence it comes
that either parents must not produce all the children
that they can, or that, if they do, the standard of
comfort in the population must deteriorate, and if
the multiplication continue, and the deterioration
augment, that the population must die off.   There
is no difficulty in showing that this assumption em-
bodies accurately enough the ordinary experience of
mankind as history records it, and as present facts
evince it.   An immense "reserve power" of multiplication is certainly to be found in most countries.
which is kept down by one obstacle or other, but
which is ready to start forward when that obstacle
is removed.   No two countries can differ more in
every respect important for this purpose than Great

Britain and British India. Yet both of them seem to prove the same result. At home, the people of Great Britain increase only at the rate of 1·01 per cent. per annum, and double in fifty-eight years; but if you take the very same population to the Colonies or the United States, it is believed to increase at a much more rapid rate, and to double itself more rapidly, though the relative increase is not nearly so great as is sometimes assumed when no sufficient account is taken of the continual immigration into those countries. The lesson of Hindostan is still more remarkable. The population of the Peninsula is ordinarily supposed not to have augmented since the time of Alexander; there is conclusive evidence that for centuries preceding the English conquest it augmented very slowly, if at all. But now, under the influence of long peace, and long good government, the population is beginning to augment very rapidly. In the North-West Provinces, where the *data* are the best, it is said to be augmenting almost as rapidly as the population of Great Britain. Here, as before, there is an immense acceleration of the rate of multiplication, because a repressive force has, as before, been withdrawn. No one can doubt that the same experiment would have a like result in other cases.

It may be said that out of Europe there is very much unoccupied land, and that even if Europe produced all the people it could, those people might be sent thither. But emigration on such a scale, though imaginable in speculation, is not possible in practice. To create very rapidly new colonies, or to

extend very rapidly old ones, requires the migration
not only of persons but of capital. You must send
thither the means of subsistence if the emigrants
are to be subsisted, and the means of employment
if they are to be employed, and capital will not go
unless you pay it. It must have its regular percentage; and as yet no capital employed in founding
colonies—no capital, that is, of a founding company,
or of founders as such—has ever paid a farthing.
The capital so expended has been a great benefit to
the emigrants and to the colony, but it has never
paid a dividend; on the contrary, the whole capital
has commonly been lost. There are no means by
which owners at home can be sure of their interest,
nor will very many owners of capital go themselves
to the colonies, only because it would much help the
poor there if they did so. Capital must be propelled
by self-interest; it cannot be enticed by benevolence.
The sudden foundation of a colony so huge as to
contain all the *possible* children—all those that might
be in excess of those which are—is impossible; the
bare idea of it is ridiculous.

Nor, if such a colony could be founded, would it
attain the end desired. Cultivated persons in Europe
do not produce all the children they might, because
they know that if they did, those children could not
lead any such life as they themselves lead. They
wish their children to have refined habits, and to
live by their talents and their mind as they do themselves. But in a colony this is simply impossible.
Rude plenty and rough prosperity are common, but
a nice refinement is all but impossible. The life of

a lady, as we see it in Europe, is in colonies impossible. As sufficient servants cannot be obtained, the mother of the family has in person to see to the manual slavery of the housework as well as look after her children, and this leaves her little opportunity for refined culture. The men are a little better off, but not much. The demand for educated labour in the colonies is exceedingly small; the business of the place is to produce corn or wool—food or raw material; neither skilled labour nor cultured labour is much wanted for that. Almost all our colonies have warned our artisans not to come thither, because there was no room; and as for the legal or other long-trained and costly mental labour of the old world, there is very little opportunity for it. Not only, therefore, is a colony impossible which should be huge enough for all the possible people of the old world, but such a colony, even if possible, would be inadequate; it would only provide for the children of rude people in the manner rude people wish; it would not provide for those of refined people in the least, as refined people wish.

The measured use of the multiplying power which is now practised by all decent people in the existing society of the old world is, therefore, more or less essential to the continuance of such a society. A use of the power without measure would certainly overcrowd such societies with high aims that could not be satisfied; and, perhaps, also with mouths which could not be fed.

And it is quite consistent with this to believe that such restraint has not at all been uniformly practised in the world, that it has been rather the rare exception, not the common rule. Such restraint has not been practised because it has not been wanted. We have been let into the secret of the matter by the experience of India. The number of the people in British India, as we have seen, was stationary for ages, but now they have begun to augment quickly. And we know the reason why.

And it is, too, quite consistent with this doctrine to believe, as has been lately urged with singular force, that we have as yet much to learn as to the theory of population,—that the numbers of all nations do not augment alike (even under seemingly similar conditions),—that there is the same difference in different families,—that there are a variety of "laws," some that can be clearly indicated, others that can be only suspected, which diminish, or seem to diminish, the multiplying capacity of mankind.

One of these is the increase of intellectual action. Physiologists say, on *a priori* ground, that if you spend nervous force in one direction, you will not have as much to spend in another. The ultimate identity of seemingly different forces is one of the most remarkable discoveries of recent science, and there is every reason to think that it applies here. An incessant action of the brain often seems to diminish the multiplying power. It can hardly be an accident that Shakespeare, Lord Bacon, Milton, Newton, and Locke—perhaps our five greatest Englishmen— had only six children between them.[1] Locke and

[1] There may be some doubt as to Newton and Shakespeare, but this is the number as far as it can be authenticated.

Newton, it is true, did not marry, but it is not irrational to suspect that the coolness of temperament which kept them single was but another phase of the same fundamental fact. But the doctrine of abstract physiology must be applied with caution; it only says that of any particular total of nervous force, what is expended in one way will not remain to be expended in another ; in any given case, to use the well-known phrase, "what is gained in children will be lost in mind"; but all cases are not alike. The nervous power of A may be fifty times that of C, and, therefore, he may do five times more brain-work than C, and also have five times his children. And, in fact, Mr. Galton finds that English judges—a strongly intellectual race as a whole—have as many children as other people. And there are some other limiting observations which might be made on the subject. Still, on the whole there seems to be a tendency in the absorbing action of intellectual power to have this particular effect, and abstract science teaches that we should expect it.

The same remark, with some limitations, is probably also applicable to women. Hardly any one who observes can doubt that women of much mind and fine nerves, as a rule, seem not so likely to have children, or, at least, not to have so many children as others. Here, too, as with men, the whole vital force in one case often may be, and often will be, different from that force in another, and, therefore, particular women may be up to the average, or even be remarkable in both ways. But still, on the whole, the existence of the tendency seems clear. And it is curiously like a similar force at the other end of the social scale. Mr. Wallace, one of the most competent of living observers, says that the increase of the population in savage tribes is much retarded by the exhausting labour of their women. And it will be a curious cycle if, as is likely in the latest civilisation, the same preventive check should again become a powerful one.

Another force which may be strongly suspected, if it cannot be quite proved, is the tendency of disheartened races and of dispirited families to die out and disappear. This force would seem to be much the same as that which operates on all wild animals when in confinement. The richest food may be given to such animals, the greatest care taken of them, and their apparent health may seem to be as good as possible, and yet they will not breed. Now all such animals are dispirited for want of the excitement of a wild life, and this may be the reason of the change in their multiplying power; at any rate, in the case of men, close observers of the dying savage races seem to think that often the mind has something to do with it. The New Zealander says that "as the English rat has supplanted the Maori rat, so the English 'man' will supplant the Maori 'man'". He looks on the extinction of his race as a fixed fate, and, in consequence, his spirits fall, his mind loses some of its tone, and his constitution some of its vigour. In civilised life particular families sometimes seem to droop and die away, though it is not possible to set down the cases exactly in figures. This is analogous to what Dr. Maudsley tells us he has observed of anxiety.

All these seem to be traces of new laws which already diminish, and in future times may still more limit, the multiplying power of mankind; but the fullest acknowledgment of them does not contradict the primary assumption made by abstract Political Economy. It will still remain true, at present, that if all people had as many children as they could, they could not provide for them as they think they ought—perhaps could not provide for them at all. Nor is it easy to imagine a future time when causes such as these should have so exceedingly diminished the sexual feelings as to make voluntary restraint of them needless. Those feelings certainly are incredibly strong now, in comparison with the forces which it is thought will hereafter supplant them. It is easy to believe that the necessity for voluntary restraint should be diminished, but it is not easy even to imagine that this necessity should be extinguished.

In the same way this primary axiom would not be impaired if it could be proved that aristocracies, as such, tend to have fewer children than other classes. Aristocracies are so small a fraction of mankind that the particular rate of their increase is not important enough to alter much the rate of increase of mankind, or even of a nation as a whole. But though this tendency of aristocracies has often been imagined, it has never been proved, and, indeed, it never will be, for it can be easily disproved. The most obvious and conclusive fact against it is that

the English aristocracy have more children than
the average of Englishmen. A common observer of
society would, indeed, expect to find this. He would
remember that the peers now differ very little from
the rest of the English gentry; that the English
gentry are, as a rule, healthy and not dissipated
men; that peers in general are married early. All
these characteristics make them likely to have more
children than other people, and, in fact, they have
more. The theory that aristocracies of necessity
diminish in number fails in this case even ludicrously,
for that theory attributes to the persons it selects
a deficiency in the very particulars in which they
were likely to excel, and do excel.

But though this assumption as to the multiplying
power of the people is true of by far the greater part
of the world, and of most ages, it is not true of all
the world or of all ages. Like the other primitive
axiom of Political Economy as to land, it fails where
" new " countries are occupied by old races. I have
already spoken of the strange chance which has un-
peopled so great a part of the world just when
civilised people wanted to go there. It is strange to
think how different would have been the fate of this
and of coming generations, if America and Australia
had possessed imperfect but thickly populated civilisations, like those of China and of India. In
climate, and in all external circumstances, America
seems as fit for an early civilisation as India.
Happily, however, it did not possess one, nor did
Australia. There is nothing there now left to
cumber the ground. A race rich in the arts of

civilisation is thus placed in a country rich in un-owned but fertile land. And in these countries there is no check on population. Those who can live there—who are the kind of people that can bear the necessary rudeness and can live there—can multiply as fast as they like; they will be able to support their children in the rough comfort of such countries; those children will not be in the least likely to die off from want or from disease; on the contrary, they will be as likely to live as any children of the human race. The possible *maximum* of multiplication is there reached, and yet none of the multipliers are deteriorated in the scale of the life, or in any of their circumstances.

And it is necessary to take most careful account of this exceptional case, because it vitally affects the present life of present commercial nations, to which Political Economy is meant to be an approxi-mation. The existence of those nations is vitally affected by the results of this exception, and there-fore those results must not be neglected. It follows from those results that Political Economy is not the " dismal science" which it was thought to be years ago, and which many people still imagine it to be. It does not teach that of necessity there will be, as time goes on, a greater and greater difficulty in providing for the increase of mankind. It assumes as an indisputable fact, a present difficulty, but it does not assume, or say, that this difficulty will in-crease. That augmentation of difficulty will not arise, first, because some of the inhabitants of old countries can emigrate to new countries, where people may increase as fast as they can; secondly, because those emigrants produce more than they want in bare subsistence, and can send home a surplus to those who remain behind; thirdly, because even in the old countries the growing improvement in the arts of production is likely, at least, to counterbalance the inevitable difficulty of a gradual resort to less favoured and fertile soils.

This short explanation will, I think, be enough to give a rude idea of the science of Political Economy in its present form. If I were writing a professed book on the science, there would be much more to be said on the subject. But I hope what has been said will be enough to make plain the rest of this book. I am to speak of the creators of Political Economy, and to criticise them, and, unless as much as this had been said, the necessary considerations could scarcely have been lucidly explained.

ADAM SMITH AND OUR MODERN ECONOMY.

I.

IF we compare Adam Smith's conception of Political Economy with that to which we are now used, the most striking point is that he never seems aware that he is dealing with what we should call an abstract science at all. *The Wealth of Nations* does not deal, as do our modern books, with a fictitious human being hypothetically simplified, but with the actual concrete men who live and move. It is concerned with Greeks and Romans, the nations of the middle ages, the Scotch and the English, and never diverges into the abstract world. Considering the natural progress of opulence as an item in greater studies, as part of the natural growth of human civilisation, Adam Smith always thought how it had been affected by human nature, taken as a whole.

Adam Smith approximates to our modern political economist, because his conception of human nature is so limited. It has been justly said that he thought "there was a Scotchman inside every man". His *Theory of Moral Sentiment*, indeed, somewhat differs in tone, but all through *The Wealth of Nations*, the desire of man to promote his pecuniary interest is treated as far more universally intense, and his willingness to labour for that interest as far

more eager and far more commonly diffused, than
experience shows them to be. Modern economists, instructed by a larger experience, well know that the
force of which their science treats is neither so potent
nor so isolated as Adam Smith thought. They
consistently advance as an assumption what he more
or less assumes as a fact.

Perhaps a little unfairly, nothing has more con-
duced to the unpopularity of modern political
economists, and to the comparative fame of Adam
Smith, than this superiority of their view over his.
Of course Adam Smith was infinitely too sensible a
man to treat the desire to attain wealth as the sole
source of human action. He much overrated its
sphere and exaggerated its effect, but he was well
aware that there was much else in human nature
besides. As a considerate and careful observer of
mankind, he could not help being aware of it.
Accordingly he often introduces references to other
motives, and describes at length and in an interesting
way what we should now consider non-economic
phenomena; and, therefore, he *is* more intelligible
than modern economists, and seems to be more
practical. But in reality he looks as if he were more
practical, only because his analysis is less complete.
He speaks as if he were dealing with all the facts of
human nature, when he is not; modern economists
know their own limitations; they would no more
undertake to prescribe for the real world, than a man
in green spectacles would undertake to describe the
colours of a landscape. But the mass of mankind
have a difficulty in understanding this. They think

Adam Smith practical because he seems to deal with all the real facts of man's life, though he actually exaggerates some, and often omits others; but they think modern economists unpractical because they have taken the most business-like step towards real practice—that of dealing with things one at a time.

And it is precisely this singular position of Adam Smith which has given him his peculiar usefulness. He fulfilled two functions. On the one hand, he prepared the way for, though he did not found, the abstract science of Political Economy. The con-ception of human nature which underlies *The Wealth of Nations* is near enough to the fictitious man of recent economic science to make its reasonings often approximate to, and sometimes coincide with, those which the stoutest of modern economists might use. The philosophical and conscious approxi-mation which we now use has been gradually framed by the continual purification of the rough and vague idea which he employed. In this way Adam Smith is the legitimate progenitor of Ricardo and of Mill. Their books would not have been written in the least as they now are, most likely would never have been written at all, unless Adam Smith, or some similar writer, had written as he has. But, on the other hand, Adam Smith is the beginner of a great practical movement too. His partial conception of human nature is near enough to the entire real truth of it to have been assumed as such in his own mind, and to be easily accepted as such by the multitude of readers. When he writes, he writes about what interests most practical men in a manner which every one will like who is able to follow any sort of written reasoning; and in his time there was a great deal of most important new truth, which most practical people were willing to learn, and which he was desirous to teach. It is difficult for a modern Englishman, to whom "Free Trade" is an accepted maxim of tedious orthodoxy, to remember sufficiently that a hundred years ago it was a heresy and a paradox. The whole commercial legislation of the world was framed on the doctrines of Protection; all financiers held them, and the practical men of the world were fixed in the belief of them. "I avow," says Monsieur Mollien, the wise Finance Minister of the first Napoleon, "to the shame of my first instructors," the previous officials of France, " that it was the book of Adam Smith, then so little known, but which was already decried by the administrators with whom I had served, which taught me better to appreciate the multitude of points at which public finance touches every family, and which raised judges of it in every household." There were many Free Traders before Adam Smith, both writers and men of business, but it is only in the antiquarian sense in which there were "poets before Homer, and kings before Agamemnon". There was no great practical teacher of the new doctrine; no one who could bring it home to the mass of men; who connected it in a plain emphatic way with the history of the past and with the facts of the present; who made men feel that it was not a mere "book theory," but a thing which might be, and ought to be, real. And thus (by a good fortune such as has hardly happened to any other writer) Adam Smith is the true parent of Mr. Cobden and the Anti-Corn Law League, as well as of Ricardo and of accurate Political Economy. His writings are semi-concrete, seeming to be quite so, and, therefore, they have been the beginning of two great movements, one in the actual, and the other in the abstract world.

Probably both these happy chances would have amazed Adam Smith, if he could have been told of them. As we have seen, the last way in which he regarded Political Economy was as a separate and confined speciality; he came upon it as an inseparable part of the development of all things, and it was in that vast connection that he habitually considered it. The peculiar mode of treating the subject which we now have, had never occurred to him. And the idea of his being the teacher, who more than any one else caused Free Trade to be accepted as the cardinal doctrine of English policy, would have been quite as strange to him. He has put on record his feeling: "To expect, indeed, that the freedom of trade should ever be entirely restored in Great Britain, is as absurd as to expect that an Oceania or Utopia should ever be established in it. Not only the prejudices of the public, but what is much more unconquerable, the private interests of many individuals, irresistibly oppose it. Were the officers of the army to oppose with the same zeal and unanimity, any reduction in the number of forces, with which master manufacturers set themselves against every law that is likely to increase the number of their rivals in the home market; were the former to animate their soldiers, in the same manner as the latter inflame their workmen, to attack with violence and outrage the proposers of any such regulation; to attempt to reduce the army would be as dangerous as it has now become to attempt to diminish in any respect the monopoly which our manufacturers have obtained against us. This monopoly has so much increased the number of some particular tribes of them, that, like an overgrown standing army, they have become formidable to the Government, and upon many occasions intimidate the legislature. The member of Parliament who supports every proposal for strengthening this monopoly is sure to acquire not only the reputation of understanding trade, but great popularity and influence with an order of men whose numbers and wealth render them of great importance. If he opposes them, on the contrary, and still more if he has authority enough to be able to thwart them, neither the most acknowledged probity, nor the highest rank, nor the greatest public services can protect him from the most infamous abuse and detraction, from personal insults, nor sometimes from real danger, arising from the insolent outrage of furious and disappointed monopolists."

Yet, in fact, the " Utopia " of Free Trade was introduced into England by the exertions of the " master manufacturers," and those who advocated it, and who were " thought to understand trade," said that they had learned the doctrines they were inculcating from *The Wealth of Nations* above and beyond every other book.

II.

If we look at *The Wealth of Nations* as if it were a book of modern Political Economy, we should ask four questions about it.

(1) What, by its teaching, is the cause which makes one thing exchange for more or less of other things?

(2) What are the laws under which that cause acts in producing these things?—the full reply to which gives the laws of population and growth of capital.

(3) If it turns ou. (as of course it does) that these things are produced by the co-operation of many people, what settles the share of each of those people in those things, or in their proceeds? The answer to this question gives what are called the laws of distribution.

(4) If this co-operation costs something (as of course it does), like all other co-operations, who is to pay that cost, and how is it to be levied? The reply to this inquiry is the theory of taxation.

To persons who have not been much accustomed to think of these subjects, these questions may seem a little strange. They will be apt to think that I ought to have spoken of the laws of wealth and of its production and distribution, rather than of the causes which make one thing exchange for more or less of other things, and of the consequent laws. But the truth is that for the purposes of Political Economy, "wealth" means that which possesses exchange value, and on that ground Archbishop Whately wanted to call the science "catallactics". The air and the sunlight—the riches of nature—are nothing in Political Economy, because every one can have them, and therefore no one will give anything for them. "Wealth" is not such for economic purposes, unless it is scarce and transferable, and so desirable that some one is anxious to give something else for it. The business of the science is not with the general bounty of nature to all men, but with the privileged possessions—bodily and mental powers included—which some have, and which others have not.

Unluckily when we come to inquire what makes these things exchange for more or less of value, one among another, we find ourselves in the middle of a question which involves many and difficult elements, and which requires delicate handling. Most of the difficulties which are felt in reflecting on the entire subject are owing to a deficient conception of the primitive ingredient. And this will surprise no one conversant with the history of science, for most errors in it have been introduced at the beginning, just as the questions which a child is apt to ask are in general the ones which it is hardest to answer.

It is usual to begin treating the subject by supposing a state of barter, and this is in principle quite right, for "money" is a peculiar commodity which requires explanation, and the simplest cases of exchange take place without it. But it is apt to be forgotten that a state of barter is not a very easy thing fully to imagine. The very simplicity which

renders it useful in speculation, makes it more and
more unlike our present complex experience. Happily, though barter has died out of the adult life of
civilised communities, there remains an age when
we, most of us, had something to do with it. To
schoolboys money is always a scarce and often a
brief possession, and they are obliged to eke out
the want by simpler expedients. The memories of
most of us may help them in the matter, though
their present life certainly will not.

Suppose, then, that one boy at school has a ham
sent him from home (those who object to trivial
illustrations must be sent back to the Platonic
Socrates to learn that they are of the most special
use in the most difficult matters, and be set to read
the history of philosophy that they may learn what
becomes of the pomposity which neglects them), and
suppose that another boy has cake, and that each
has more of his own than he cares for and lacks
something of the other, what are the proportions
in which they will exchange ? If boy A likes his
own ham scarcely at all, or not very much, and if he
is very fond of cake, he will be ready to barter a
great deal of it against a little of boy B's cake ; and
if boy B is fond of cake too and does not care so
much for ham, cake will be at a premium, and a
very little of it will go a great way in the transaction,
especially if the cake is a small one and the ham a
big one ; but if, on the contrary, both boys care
much for ham, and neither much for cake, and also
the ham be small and the cake large, then the ham
will be at a premium, the cake at a discount, and

both sides of the exchange will be altered.   The use
of this simplest of all cases is that you see the
inevitable complexity of, and that you cannot
artificially simplify, the subject.   There are in every
exchange, as we here see, no less than six elements
which more or less affect it in general; first, the
quantities of the two commodities, and next, two
feelings in each exchanger—first, his craving for the
commodity of the other, and secondly, his liking or
disinclination for his own.   In every transaction,
small or great, you will be liable to blunder unless
you consider all six.

The introduction of money introduces in this
respect no new element.   The inseparable use of
that incessant expedient is that which ingrains into
civilised life the abstract idea of a "purchasing
power"; of a thing which, when possessed, will
obtain all other things.   And independently of the
hand-to-hand use of money, this idea of it as a
universal equivalent, with the consequent means
of counting, has been incalculably beneficial to
civilisation.   But into a mere single interchange
its use introduces nothing new.   Money, in that
aspect, is simply a desirable commodity; it often
happens to be particularly coveted, but at other
times, in comparison with some simpler and more
essential things, its worth is insignificant.

Nor do the common bargains of commerce contain
any additional ingredient.   There are always six
things to be considered.   Suppose that a holder of
£10,000 "Peruvians" wants to sell them on the
London Exchange, the price he will get will obvi-

ously vary with the quantity of Peruvian stock there is about in the market, and the quantity of money which the owners are ready to invest in it; but also according to four other things.

First,—Whether he is anxious for money or not; if he has a bill to meet to-morrow morning and must have money, the chances are great that some one will take advantage of his necessities, and he will have to take less; if, on the other hand, he be a rich man—a strong holder, as the phrase is—he will say, "Ah, if I cannot get my price to-day I will wait till to-morrow," and so he will get a better price.

Secondly,—Even if he is not violently in want of money, the price will vary according as he thinks "Peruvians" more or less likely to fall or not. If he thinks them a declining or "treacherous" stock, he will be anxious to get rid of them, and will be less difficult as to price; if he had private and peculiar knowledge that Peru was about to imitate Spain and to stop payment the next day, he will sell at once for any price that those not in the secret would be ready to give him. In these two ways the bargain would be influenced by the mental state of the seller, and it will be influenced in two ways also by the mental state of the buyer.

Thirdly,—If the buyer is desirous of the article, because he thinks it will get rapidly up, he of course will give more than if he thinks it is likely to be stationary, or even for a time to fall. He will "discount" the prospect of improvement, as the market phrase has it.

Fourthly,—If he can make little of his money

in other ways, say, if it is earning 2 per cent., he will be ready to put it into " Peruvians " at a much lower price than he would if he could get 7 per cent. for it in other ways. If there were a crisis, and money had risen in value to 10 per cent., he would hardly put it out of his own control by buying " Peruvians " with it, at any price, no matter how low. He would prize the money at such a time, because in a general disturbance it may often be used to untold advantage, or may save its owner from ruin.

In the bargains in all other commodities the same considerations have to be taken account of, and no others. A bargain in foreign stocks or railway shares is in essentials the same as one in corn or cheese. The same six elements are in each case to be thought of, and no others.

Every transaction in commerce is in a legal sense separate ; it is a contract in which one side engages to do certain things in return for certain other things which are to be done by the other side. But in a practical sense most important commercial pheno- mena are interlaced one with another. The feelings of each seller as to parting, or not parting, with his goods, are mainly caused—or much caused at any rate—by the amount of goods which other dealers have now in or are about to bring to market, and also by what he imagines to be their " strength " or " weakness "; that is, their more or less of inclination to part with their goods or to retain them in every market, and a most able living economist [1] has justly

---

[1] Professor Jevons' *Theory of Political Economy*, page 84.

observed that now-a-days this is what we mean by
" a market"; the estimate formed of all which the
dealers have, and of all which they expect to have,
is all pretty much collected into one corporate
opinion, which floats variously about upon the lips of
men, though often it would not be easy to condense
into a formula, or to bring it home on evidence to
any single speaker. For the most part it is an im-
bibed, not a discovered, fact, that the market is
" dull, and likely to be dull," " lively, and likely to
be so ". These are in part truths of observation,
but in part also accredited hypotheses. A market
knows its own present state, and anticipates its own
future, by signs which an outside observer would not
see, and by the unconscious contribution of many
minds to a daily growing opinion. A market in the
higher commercial sense of the word—in the sense
in which we speak of the " money market"—does
not mean, as it once did, a place where goods were
exposed, but an historical result of the proximity of
traders, a set of dealers cognisant of one another,
and acquainted more or less with each other's
position, and each other's intentions.

It must not be supposed, however, that the process
of bargain-making approaches in general to a
statistical calculation. A person proposing to buy,
looks at a trade circular to see what the writer of it
thinks the price is; he asks the broker what price
has been given, what offered, what refused; he
inquires whether holders are strong or weak, whether
they are under supplied or over supplied; he asks if
other buyers are many or few, whether they are eager

or indifferent, whether they have much money, or whether they have little; and out of these inquiries he forms an idea of the price at which he is likely to buy the commodities. A person intending to sell a commodity forms in like manner a notion of the price he is likely to obtain for it; on the surface the appearance is often frivolous enough. Many persons go about inquiring, " In what state do you think the market, sir ? " and getting, as it would seem, not much reply in return. But underneath there are some of the keenest anxieties and most ardent hopes of human nature. A large quantity of goods is on the market, by selling which many holders must live, if they live at all. A great, though uncertain, quantity of money is in the market, which the owners mean to live by investing. The main interest of many lives is at stake, and the subsistence of many families, little as on the outside the market looks so.

On the whole, then, we may sum the matter up thus :—

Firstly,—That a bargain will be struck when four conditions are satisfied, *viz.* :—

" When the seller thinks he cannot obtain more from the buyer with whom he is dealing, or from any other;

" When he is sufficiently desirous to sell his article, or enough in want of money to take that price ;

" When the buyer thinks that he cannot obtain the article for less, either from that seller or from any one else ;

" When he is so eager for the article, or so anxious to invest his money, as to give it."

Secondly,—That every bargain is a datum for other bargains, and influences the opinions on which they are based.

Thirdly,—That the average price of such bargains is the market price.

Fourthly,—That the main elements of market price are those which prevail in most bargains, *viz.*, the actual quantity of the article in the market, the quantity of money actually ready to be invested in it, and the average strength with which the wish to hold the article, the wish to acquire it, the wish to obtain money, and the wish to invest it, operate through the whole class of buyers and of sellers.

These formulæ may seem complex, but I do not think that any of them can be left out or shortened except by omitting necessary facts. [1]

An attempt is, indeed, commonly made to abbreviate these rules. Very much the same is meant by the common phrase that market price is determined by " supply and demand," which is a good phrase enough when you know how to manage it. But the effect of using so few words for so much meaning is that they are continually being used in various senses; no one signification of the terms can be stretched over the whole matter. And in consequence a literature has come to exist discussing their ambiguities. The most obvious objection is hat, if the w ords are taken in their natural sense, they imply a relation between two things of wholly different natures ; demand is a desire in the mind,

---

[1] See Note A on Market Price at the end of the volume.

supply a quantity of matter; how then can there be an equality between them ? And even when demand is used in the best sense,[1] for the quantity of money or purchasing power, the formula has the defect of mentioning only the two quantities of the changing commodities, of not saying that they are only estimates of quantities, and of not warning those who use it that they must likewise consider the other elements—the four wishes of the two exchangers.

It is most important to be clear upon the matter, because confusion about it has led, and still leads, to many most mischievous fallacies. For example, it has been vigorously argued that " Trades Unions " could not alter the price of labour. " The supply, the number of labourers," it was said, " is the same as before, and also the demand, *viz.*, the quantity of money wanting to buy labour—the two causes being thus identical, the effect cannot be different." But, in fact, a Trades Union establishment at once alters the mental conditions. It turns the labourer, in the Stock Exchange language, from a weak holder into a strong one; it enables him to hold. Before, he must either take the master's terms or starve ; now, he has money to live, and will often get more, be-cause he can stand out for a good bargain.

The complete view of the facts thus effaces at once the ingrained mistake of the last generation.

[1] See the admirable dissertation of Professor Cairnes, *Leading Principles*, pages 17-40. A most ingenious collec-tion of the difficulties of the doctrine of supply and demand as usually stated, will be found in *Thornton on Labour*, book ii. cap. I.

and it also destroys as quickly a recent error now common. It is imagined that because Trades Unions have sometimes raised wages to some extent, they can raise them, at any rate gradually, to any extent. But we now see the limit of their power. They can only win when the funds of the Union are stronger than the funds of the capitalists; and this will sometimes be so, and sometimes not be so. A clear view of the facts also explains (that which is a difficulty in the ordinary theory) the difference between a speculative market and an ordinary one. So long as it is imagined that market price is determined by the supply of the article in the market, and the money here eager to buy it, it is not possible to explain why two markets in which both these elements coincide should be so different as a dull market and an excited one always are. But as soon as we understand that we have to deal likewise with opinions and with wishes, we see how there is great scope for discrepancy and for mutability.

Again, on another side of the subject, it has been incessantly said that (at all events since the Act of 1844, which limits the power of issue) the Bank of England cannot alter the rate of discount. There exists, it is said, a certain number of bills, and a certain amount of money ready to be invested in bills, and this determines the way in which one will be exchanged for the other. But, in fact, much of such money is held by the Bank of England, and the fact of its being unwilling to lend, inevitably alters "the equation of exchange". The desire of the principal dealers to operate, or not to operate, is a vital element in every market. When you read in the jargon of trade circulars that "yarns are sluggish, and that teas are lively," the palliation for the use of these ridiculous adjectives is that in the facts described there is as much of mental state as of physical supply.

It is in consequence of the extreme importance of these mental elements that in all markets you hear so much of "flying and often concocted rumours". On the Stock Exchange "the lie of the day," as Dr. Johnson would have called it, always has some influence, because the momentary wishes of sellers to sell, and buyers to buy, are greatly affected by what they hear as to possible wars and revolutions of the nations whose debts they are buying and selling. The best States only care for such rumours at critical instants, but more or less the repute of minor ones lies at the "truth of him that makes it," and their credit is incessantly talked up and talked down much more than they themselves desire.

The league of the moment—"rig," "ring," "syndicate," or "pool," or what not—"one form with many names"—operates in the same way. It is a mental expedient for changing the mental state of the market. By combining, the same persons are able to make the same amount of speech and the same amount of money go farther. They affect opinion more, because they say the same things, and they are more tenacious holders, or more desperate buyers, because they rely one on another.

We see, too, from this analysis why it is that one man is a good seller and another a bad one A good seller is a good advocate, who acts effectually on the opinions and feelings of persons inclined to deal with him, who makes them think that the article is very excellent, that it is growing very scarce, that it is going to be scarcer, that a great many people are wanting it, that much money is going to be had for it, that the holders in general are anxious not to sell as yet because they believe it will get dearer, that he himself is above all unwilling to part with his article and will do so only as a personal favour. He weakens the judgment and intensifies the desire of his opponent as he wishes.

The requisites of a good buyer are in essentials the same. He also is an advocate, only on the other side. He has to show that the article in question is undesirable, that it is plentiful, that most holders are most anxious to sell it, that few persons, and those with little money, are coming forward to buy it, that though, perhaps, he might himself be induced to buy a little of it, yet it would only be under peculiar circumstances, and as a matter of private feeling. There is, indeed, a common saying that a good buyer is much rarer than a good seller ; and I believe that the Manchester warehouse-keepers, as they are called—that is, the great dealers in underclothing,—great traders, but who do not produce anything, and must therefore both largely buy and sell—give higher salaries to their buyers than to their sellers. But this is only because the buyers are the advocates who have to address the more skilled audience. They buy of a few manufacturers who understand business well, and must, therefore, be careful what they say. The sellers for the firm, who distribute the goods among the country shops, have people of very inferior intelligence to deal with. A few good buyers, therefore, purchase what many less qualified sellers dispose of. But in its essence the business is identical. It consists in exciting desire and in modifying opinion.

It may strike some people that if prices thus depend on casual opinions and on casual desires, it is odd that prices in markets should be so uniform on particular days in particular markets as they really are. But in fact, at ordinary times, these casual opinions and casual desires form a sort of average. The timid seller is emboldened by knowing that others are courageous; the necessitous by knowing that others are strong; the cautious buyer is forced on because he knows that eager ones will outstrip him; the adventurous is restrained because he knows that others have doubts, and so on through the whole subject. In the infancy of trade no doubt there is ample room for great variations. A most graphic observer[1] has said of Oriental markets: "The necessities of a savage are soon satisfied, and unless he belong to a nation civilised enough to live in permanent habitations, and secure from plunder, he cannot accumulate, but is only able to keep what he is actually able to carry about his own person. Thus, the chief at Lake N'gomi told Mr. Andersson

---

[1] Galton's *Art of Travel*, under "Presents and Articles for Payment".

that his beads would be of little use, for the women about the place already 'grunted like pigs' under the burden of those that they wore, and which they had received from previous travellers."

In civilised times facts are known, advocacy is weak, and prices are usually uniform. But they are not so at a commercial crisis; then, as the phrase goes, prices are very " wide ". A necessitous seller must sell, and he pulls down the price for an instant, but if a buyer is stimulated by this, and wants to buy more at the same price, he will find that he cannot do it. There are no more equally necessitous sellers in the market; the rest do not want money for the instant, and will not sell, except at a much higher price. At such a moment, too, skilful people will act on the fears of others. I have heard it said of a bland and delicate operator, who was ultimately very successful, that at critical times " he *encouraged* others to be frightened ". And in panics cool heads and strong nerves make much by dealing with weak nerves and hot heads. But in common times the contrary tendencies are subdued to an average. The most anxious seller will depress a good stock but very little, and the most eager will raise it but a little also.

I have been obliged to state the facts carefully, before discussing Adam Smith's doctrine, because I could not otherwise make an attempt to estimate it intelligibly, and I must go on with some further facts also, or even that estimate would be broken and faulty. At a glance it is plain that the doctrine of exchange which I have sketched, cannot be the final

theory. It depends on the relative quantity of two
things, but as most things can be increased at will
by human labour, men have, therefore, in most cases
the means of making these quantities what they
please, and therefore these quantities cannot be
ultimate causes. "Supply and demand" cannot be
final regulators of value, for in most cases men can
supply what they like, and to finish the subject we
must know when they will begin to do so, and when
they will leave off.

The first answer to be given to these questions
s, that producers who produce in order to receive
something in exchange for their products, will go on
producing as long as the gain, pleasure, satisfaction
(whatever word you choose to use) they receive from
that something is a sufficient compensation to them
for the *bore* and irksomeness of production, and they
will stop producing when it ceases to be sufficient.
In an early state of society it is easy to imagine
simple cases of this. In the times of which the
Scandinavian "kitchenmiddings" are the only extant
vestige, the population lived partly by hunting and
partly by fishing; most, I suppose, did both; some
confined themselves to that which they did best. In
that case a hunter, who only hunted, would work as
long as the fish received in exchange seemed to him
to repay the trouble of hunting; a fisherman, who
only fished, would do the same. The man who tat-
tooed the population would continue to do so as long
as the game or the fish he received in return seemed
to make it worth his while. The polisher of flint
implements or bones would do just the same. The

essence of the whole is the exchange of the produce of much labour and very little capital, so long as the labourer thinks what he thus obtains repays him for his labour. And the same thing goes on down to the end of civilisation in a subordinate way. An old woman gathers laver on the sea-shore of Somersetshire as long as any one will give the pittance she expects for it. A diver will bring up pearls as long as any one will give what he thinks is enough to make it worth while to go to the bottom of the sea for them. The primitive form of production still exists, and the primitive estimate of recompense, but in most cases they exist as "survivals" only. In two remarkable instances, of which I shall speak hereafter, they still alter the main tide of commerce. But for the most part the interest of the transactions is principally antiquarian; little money is now made by them, but they are worth thinking of now and then, because they remind us of what once was the only way in which the relative value of commodities was finally determined in the world.

The main part of modern commerce is carried on in a very different manner. It begins at a different point, and ends at a different point. The fundamental principle is, indeed, the same; the determining producer—the person on whose volition it depends whether the article shall be produced or not—goes on so long as he is satisfied with his recompense, and stops when he ceases to be so satisfied. But this determining producer is now not a labourer but a capitalist. In nine hundred and ninety-nine cases out of every thousand, it is the capitalist and not the labourer who decides whether or not an enterprise shall be commenced, and therefore whether the consequent commodity shall come on the market. He buys his labour just as he buys his raw material; he may calculate wrongly in both cases, he may think he will buy when labour or material is cheaper than it turns out that he can; but his calculation will be the critical element in the whole business; that which decides whether it shall or shall not be entered upon.

This change has occurred in the organisation of industry, because the new mode of organising it is infinitely more efficient than the old. A body of separate labourers has many of the characteristics of a mob; but one acting under the control of a capitalist has many of those of an army. A capitalist provides his labourers with subsistence, directs each what he shall do and when, and educes the desired result of the whole combination at the proper time, much as a general does. He and his men will live and will produce riches where a mere multitude of labourers will starve. When, in very modern times, it has been endeavoured in schemes of "co-operation" to enable labourers to subsist without dependence on an individual capitalist, it has been necessary, under cloak of the combination, to invent a capitalist in disguise. A common fund subscribed beforehand, an elected board to invest it, a selected manager to combine it, are all refined expedients for doing in a complex way what the single rich capitalist does in a simple way; even yet we do not know how far they can be applied with comparable efficiency. In simpler times the rich man who has much beforehand, buys the labour of his poorer neighbours who have nothing, and directs their power towards results which no one of them could perhaps have conceived, and which a thousand times as many, without his controlling mind, would have been impotent to produce. On one point, however, the point which is most material for the present purpose, the old organisation, or disorganisation, of mere labourers acting separately, and the exact modern industry, where enterprise depends on the *fiat* of the capitalist, are alike; and are so because human nature is alike both in capitalist and labourer. Neither of them will take much trouble to obtain in one way that which he can obtain with very little trouble in another way. As far as labour can migrate from employment to employment, articles produced by the same labour will exchange for one another. If it were not so, the labourers who worked at the thing which fetched least would be throwing away some of their labour; they would do better to produce something else, and in the end they would do so. In the same way, as far as capital (including the capital which buys labour) can be transferred from employment to employment, things produced with the same amount of capital, in similar times and similar circumstances, exchange one for another. When it is not so, capital tends to go from the pursuit in which it is less profitably employed to those in which it is more so.

As might be expected, the modern organisation is much more perfect in this respect as in most others. Labour always circulates from employment to employment. "Whatever," says Adam Smith, "obstructs the free circulation of labour from one employment to another, obstructs that of stock likewise; the quantity of stock which can be employed in any branch of business depending very much upon that of the labour which can be employed in it. Corporation laws, however, give less obstruction to the free circulation of stock from one place to another than to that of labour. It is everywhere much easier for a wealthy merchant to obtain the privilege of trading in a town corporate, than for a poor artificer to obtain that of working in it. The obstruction which corporation laws give to the free circulation of labour is common, I believe, to every part of Europe. That which is given to it by the poor laws is, so far as I know, peculiar to England. It consists in the difficulty which a poor man finds in obtaining a settlement, or even in being allowed to exercise his industry in any parish but that to which he belongs. It is not the labour of artificers and manufacturers only of which the free circulation is obstructed by corporation laws. The difficulty of obtaining settlements obstructs even that of common labour."

Man is of all pieces of luggage the most difficult to be removed. In general an ill-paid labourer early in life gives hostages to misfortune, he burdens himself with the support of a wife and children; he cannot move, or they would starve. But civilisation has invented an elaborate machinery for holding capital in a transferable form. The basis of this machinery is the invention of money. One of the uses of money is that it is a mode in which capital may be held without loss in what may be called a provisional form. All capital originally comes from production—is, say, so much corn, or tin, or hemp—but if a man holds corn, or any other commodity, he may not be able to exchange it in a little while for so much as he can to-day. Most commodities are in their nature perishable, and most others are liable to depreciation from the change in human desires. But money is always wanted, for it will buy everything; any one who is not sure how he will ultimately employ his capital can hold it in the form of money. This provisional state—this interval of non-employment—is a great security for the substantial equality of equal capitals in equal employments, for it gives capitalists time to look before them and see what they should select because it will yield most, and what they should avoid because it will yield least.

But in this, its elementary form, the machinery for holding capital, so to say, in expectation, has an obvious defect; the capitalists derive no income from it while it is in a state of indecision. " Money is barren," according to the old saying, and whoever holds mere coin will certainly derive no income. But in countries where banking is well developed, the machinery is far more efficient; a man who has capital lying idle can place it with a banker, who, if he will agree to give some notice before he withdraws it, will agree to pay him some interest on it. This interest, as far as it goes, is a source of income during the period of suspended investment, and is something on which the capitalist can subsist without trenching on his capital, and without hurrying

to a premature use of it.   This capital awaiting investment the banker employs in the same way that
he employs the unused balances of people's income,
and that is in lending to the trades which are at the moment most profitable.   As I have elsewhere explained:
" Political Economists say that capital sets towards
the most profitable trades, and that it rapidly leaves
the less profitable and non-paying trades.   But in
ordinary countries this is a slow process, and some
persons who want to have ocular demonstration of
abstract truths have been inclined to doubt it,
because they could not see it.   In England, however, the process would be visible enough if you
could only see the books of the bill brokers and the
bankers.   Their bill cases as a rule are full of the
bills drawn in the most profitable trades, and, *cæteris
paribus*, in comparison empty of those drawn in the
less profitable.   If the iron trade ceases to be as
profitable as usual, less iron is sold ; the fewer the
sales the fewer the bills ; and in consequence the
number of iron bills in Lombard Street is diminished.
On the other hand, if in consequence of a bad
harvest the corn trade becomes on a sudden profitable, immediately ' corn bills ' are created in great
numbers, and, if good, are discounted in Lombard
Street.   Thus English capital runs as surely and
instantly where it is most wanted, and where there
is most to be made of it, as water runs to find its
level."

    In this way " expectant capital," while it is so ex-
pectant, forms part of a fund which is lent now to
this trade, and now to that, according as for the

moment each trade is more profitable; and at last instructed by reflection, its owner will invest it, other things being equal, in the trade which offers the most for it. In its temporary use it tends to equalise temporary profits; in its permanent use it does so too.

No doubt some callings are naturally pleasant, others unpleasant; some encouraged by opinion, others adverse to it; some easy to learn, some difficult; some easy to enter, others hedged in by tradition and privilege; some abounding in risk, some with little of it. But our principle is not affected by these. It is that, non-pecuniary encouragements and discouragements being reckoned, capitals employed in all trades yield an equal return in equal times.

What that return will be it would be premature here to speak of. It is only necessary to say that it is such as the capitalist will think worth while to invest his capital for, enough, that is, to compensate him for the inevitable trouble and attendant risk; if it is not enough he will let it continue uninvested at interest, or will eat it up and live on it.

We must carefully bear in mind, too, that the rule that equivalent returns are made to equal capitals in the same times, is only true of employments between which capital fluctuates freely. This is to an almost perfect extent true of employments in this country, and to a great extent, though far from an equal extent, to all employments within their own country. But it is not at all true of employments in different countries; English capital, by far the most

locomotive of all capitals, will not go abroad for the
same percentage of return. that will suffice it at
home. A great deal of the capital of all countries—
by far the greater part of it everywhere, indeed—could
hardly on any terms be tempted abroad. We have
arrived, however, at the principle that within the
same nation all commodities will tend to be of the
same exchangeable value, whose cost of production
is identical, and that this cost of production is that
which the capitalist expends, and the return for
which he is willing to take the pains of expending it.

And this will be enough for our present purpose.

III.

On all these subjects Adam Smith wrote in an
extinct world, and one of the objects always before
him was to destroy now extinct superstitions. In
that age it was still believed, though the belief was
dwindling away, that wealth consisted in "money,"
and that its value was somehow different from that
of anything else. As Adam Smith himself describes
it: "That wealth consists in money, or in gold and
silver, is a popular notion which naturally arises from
the double function of money, as the instrument of
commerce, and as the measure of value. In consequence of its being the instrument of commerce,
when we have money we can more readily obtain
whatever else we have occasion for than by means
of any other commodity. The great affair, we
always find, is to get money. When that is obtained,
there is no difficulty in making any subsequent pur-

chase. In consequence of its being the measure of value, we estimate that of all other commodities by the quantity of money which they will exchange for. We say of a rich man that he is worth a great deal, and of a poor man that he is worth very little money. A frugal man, or a man eager to be rich, is said to love money; and a careless, a generous, or a profuse man, is said to be indifferent about it. To grow rich is to get money; and wealth and money, in short, are, in common language, considered as in every respect synonymous."

No true theory of "value" could be established till this false theory was cleared away. So long as even a vestige of it haunts the minds of thinkers and learners, they cannot think or learn anything on this subject properly. And therefore Adam Smith applied his whole force to the confutation of it. His success has been so complete that it has made this part of his writings now useless. No one now thinks or supposes that money is the essence of wealth; that it is anything but a kind of wealth, having distinct uses, like other kinds. The strongest interest in reading the chapters of *The Wealth of Nations* on the subject is given by the vigour with which they are written. They are essentially models of practical writing; they are meant to extirpate living error; they follow that error into the minds of those who believe it, and extirpate it in the forms in which it thrives and rules there. The error that the precious metals are the only real wealth, was a living error to Adam Smith, for he had lived with many persons who held it.

The efficacy of Adam Smith's refutation is not wholly derived exactly from its literary merit. Hume had before given a brief exposure, which in mere writing is at least as good. But Hume impressed on this, as on so much else, a certain taint of paradox. He seems to be playing with his subject; he hardly appears to believe what he says, and a plain reader is often puzzled to know whether he ought to believe it either. On a strong-headed man of business, semi-insincere exposition produces no effect. But Adam Smith takes up the subject in a solid, straightforward way, such as he knew would suit the Glasgow merchants with whom he had once lived, and he talks to them, not only as a man acquainted with present mercantile things, but also as one possessing much other culture and authority. He impressed practical men by his learning, at the same time that he won them by his lucidity and assured them by his confidence.

But when we pass from the refutation of ancient errors to the establishment of coherent truth, we shall not be equally satisfied. Students are, indeed, still sometimes told that they will find such truth in Adam Smith, but those who had nothing else to read, and who wanted to read accurately, did not find it so. What in fact a student will find in Adam Smith is a rough outline of sensible thoughts; not always consistent with themselves, and rarely stated with much precision; often very near the truth, though seldom precisely hitting it; a great mental effort in its day, though always deficient in the consecutiveness required by careful learners, and, except for the purpose of exciting an interest in the subject, altogether superseded and surpassed now.

"Gold and silver, however," says Adam Smith, "like every other commodity, vary in their value, are sometimes cheaper and sometimes dearer, sometimes of easier and sometimes of more difficult purchase. The quantity of labour which any particular quantity of them can purchase or command, or the quantity of other goods which it will exchange for, depends always upon the fertility or barrenness of the mines which happen to be known about the time when such exchanges are made. The discovery of the abundant mines of America reduced in the sixteenth century the value of gold and silver in Europe to about a third of what it had been before. As it cost less labour to bring those metals from the mine to the market, so when they were brought thither they could purchase or command less labour ; and this revolution in their value, though perhaps the greatest, is by no means the only one of which history gives some account. But as a measure of quantity, such as the natural foot, fathom, or handful, which is continually varying in its own quantity, can never be an accurate measure of the quantity of other things ; so a commodity which is itself continually varying in its own value can never be an accurate measure of the value of other commodities. Equal quantities of labour, at all times and places, may be said to be of equal value to the labourer. In his ordinary state of health, strength and spirits, in the ordinary degree of his skill and dexterity, he must always lay down the same portion of his ease, his liberty, and his happiness. The price which he pays must always be the same, whatever may be the quantity of goods which he receives in return for it. Of these, indeed, it may sometimes purchase a greater and sometimes a smaller quantity; but it is their value which varies, not that of the labour which purchases them. At all times and places that is dear which it is difficult to come at, or which it costs much labour to acquire; and that cheap which is to be had easily, or with very little labour. Labour alone, therefore, never varying in its own value, is alone the ultimate and real standard by which the value of all commodities can at all times and places be estimated and compared. It is their real price; money is their nominal price only."

But in the present day it is not true at all that things are dear simply in proportion to the mere labour which it has cost to produce them. A thousand men's labour assisted, say, by ten steam-engines, will produce many more valuable things than a thousand men's labour without those steam-engines. The result of the labour of the two sets of men will not exchange for one another at all. Besides immediate labour there is a vast apparatus of the assisting results of past labour. These must be paid for in some way, or their owner will not let them be used. There is something else essential to modern industry besides labour, and that is *saving*, or the refraining from the immediate consumption of past labour. Sometimes this saving is used to co-operate with labour, as in machines, sometimes to support it, as with food and necessaries. But in either case its existence must be remunerated, and its use paid for. As modern economists say, the value of an article must be such as to compensate not only for the labour, but for the *abstinence* by which it was produced.

Again,—Adam Smith speaks of the quantity of labour which a commodity will buy, as if it were identical with the quantity of labour by which it was produced. He says: "Every man is rich or poor according to the degree in which he can afford to enjoy the necessaries, conveniences, and amusements of human life. But after the division of labour has once thoroughly taken place, it is but a very small part of these with which a man's own labour can supply him. The far greater part of them he must derive from the labour of other people, and he must be rich or poor according to the quantity of that labour which he can command, or which he can afford to purchase. The value of any commodity, therefore, to the person who possesses it, and who means not to use or consume it himself, but to exchange it for other commodities, is equal to the quantity of labour which it enables him to purchase or command. Labour, therefore, is the real measure of the exchangeable value of all commodities. The real price of everything, what everything really costs to the man who wants to acquire it, is the toil and trouble of acquiring it. What everything is really worth to the man who has acquired it, and who wants to dispose of it or exchange it for something else, is the toil and trouble which it can save to himself, and which it can impose upon other people. What is bought with money or with goods is purchased by labour, as much as what we acquire by the toil of our own body. That money or those goods indeed save us this toil. They contain the value of a certain quantity of labour which we exchange for what is supposed at the time to contain the value of an equal quantity. Labour was the first price, the original purchase money that was paid for all things. It was not by gold or by silver, but by labour, that all the wealth of the world was originally purchased; and its value, to those who possess it, and who want to exchange it for some new productions, is precisely equal to the quantity of labour which it can enable them to purchase or command."

But the quantity of labour which a thing will purchase depends on the degree in which it is desired by labourers. A grand piano in a coarse community will buy less labour than a barrel of beer. Mere labour is the worst " measure " of value conceivable, because it varies with the appetites and differs with the tastes of mankind. There is nothing more uncertain, more changeable, or more casual than the number of days' labour that an article will purchase. As some one expressed it : " Gin will purchase more than it ought, and tracts less than they ought ".

Adam Smith did not put the matter graphically enough before his mind. He speaks of a man's fortune being equal " to the quantity either of other men's labour, *or what is the same thing*, of the produce of other men's labour which it enables him to command ". But unless you suppose that some general instrument of purchasing power, like money, exists, and that a man's fortune consists in it, the two things are not the same at all. One man's fortune may consist of a valuable library, which would buy no manual labour at all, but for which bookish people would barter many other commodities; another may have a heap of coarse meat and drink, which will bring crowds of labourers to share them, but for which few refined persons would give anything.

Unquestionably, as has been shown, in a rude state of society, where labour is the principal cost of production, two articles produced with the same amounts of labour will tend to exchange one for another because every labourer will tend to migrate to the place where his labour is better rewarded, and leave the place where it is worse. And this is what Adam Smith vaguely saw, and several times meant to say, but he did not exactly say it; he never says it, and often says something quite different.

In another passage Adam Smith sets forth a similarly vague view of the doctrine of exchangeable value as it stands after capital has accumulated. But, as will be shown, he does not work it out fully, and he does not reconcile it, or feel that there is a difficulty in reconciling it, with his former doctrine of value based on mere labour, and yet they are plainly incompatible. "There is," he says, " in every society or neighbourhood an ordinary or average rate both of wages and profit in every different employment of labour and stock. This rate is naturally regulated, as I shall show hereafter, partly by the general circumstances of the society, their riches or poverty, their advancing, stationary or declining condition, and partly by the particular nature of each employment. There is likewise in every society or neighbourhood an ordinary or average rate of rent, which is regulated too, as I shall show hereafter, partly by the general circumstances of the society or neighbourhood in which the land is situated, and partly by the natural or improved fertility of the land. These ordinary or average rates may be called the natural rates of wages, profit, and rent, at the time and place in which they commonly prevail. When the price of any commodity is neither more nor less than what is sufficient to pay the rent of the land, the wages of the labour, and the profits of the stock employed in raising, preparing, and bringing it to market, according to their natural rates, the commodity is then sold for what may be called its natural price. The commodity is then sold precisely for what it is worth, or for what it really costs the person who brings it to market; for though in common language what is called the prime cost of any commodity does not comprehend the profit of the person who is to sell it again, yet if he sells it at a price which does not allow him the ordinary rate of profit in his neighbourhood, he is evidently a loser by the trade; since by employing his stock in some other way he might have made that profit. His profit, besides, is his revenue, the proper fund of his subsistence. As, while he is preparing and bringing the goods to market, he advances to his workmen their wages, or their subsistence; so he advances to himself, in the same manner, his own subsistence, which is generally suitable to the profit which he may reasonably expect from the sale of his goods. Unless they yield him this profit, therefore, they do not repay him what they may very properly be said to have really cost him. Though the price, therefore, which leaves him this profit, is not always the lowest at which a dealer may sometimes sell his goods, it is the lowest at which he is likely to sell them for any considerable time; at least where there is perfect liberty, or where he may change his trade as often as he pleases."

As every one will see, this second doctrine is much more like real life than the former. But in Adam Smith's mind it did not supersede it. All through *The Wealth of Nations* there is recurring confusion between three things, the "natural price" of an article estimated as in the above passage, the quantity of labour required to make it, and the quantity of labour which it will buy; of which three things no one ever for the most part coincides with the others.

Even this second exposition contains one error, which unfits it for scientific use, and which the sharp eye of Hume at once perceived. " I cannot think," Hume wrote, " that the rent of farms makes any part of the price of produce. " And very clearly it does not. For, if it does, of what farm ? The rent of various pieces of corn-growing land varies infinitely; is it the rent of the dearest which enters

into the price of the half-and-half, or of the cheapest?
We know that the price of corn is the same, no
matter on what quality of land it is grown.   Does
that price pay the rent of good, of indifferent, or of
bad land?   This question Adam Smith does not
answer, nor seemingly does the necessity of answering it occur to him.

On the other hand, it must be owned that there is
a great naturalness in Adam Smith's idea.   It is
that which would strike every one on a first view of
the facts.   The capitalist pays the rent of the land,
just as he pays the wages and buys the seed corn;
and it is as much necessary that he should be recouped for the payment of that rent as for either of
the other payments.   If the "rent" of the farm is
not an element in the price of the corn, how then is
that rent to be paid?

The answer is, that the rent of extra good land is
paid out of the extra quantity (or extra good quality)
of what it produces.   If one acre of land yields twice
as much as another, it will answer the capitalist's
purpose to pay twice as much for its use.   But if he
does pay twice as much, the cost at which he will
grow each ear of corn will be the same as that of the
farmer on less good land; the extra fertility will be
compensated by the extra rent.   It may, of course,
be that the owner of the best land will farm it himself, and then he will have no rent to pay for its unusual goodness.   But he will not sell his produce
the least cheaper for that; he will get all that he
can for it.   We have seen how "market price" is
determined: it depends on certain desires of the

seller and the buyer, in part generated by the quantity of the article and the quantity of money, and in part not. But none of those desires would make a man say: " I produce this at a less cost than others, and therefore I will let them charge a higher price than I do ". No producer sets himself to introduce fairness into the reward of production, by letting those who possessed less facilities than he did, receive more than he does. The nature of market-going man is formed quite differently.

The only reason why the cost of production in the end tends to determine market value is that every one who wants an article will take the easiest means to get it. If a capitalist wants to invest his money to gain an income, he will, *cæteris paribus*, be apt to engage in pursuits which are reputed profitable, and to avoid those which are reputed unprofitable; and this will reduce the profits of all trades not *to* a level, but *towards* a level. But the argument assumes that all means of production are equally open to every one. If any one has exclusive possession of an especially good opportunity, he will get something out of it proportioned to that especial goodness. The owner of extremely good land, who farms it himself, will get a return over and above the ordinary rate of profit in propoition to that goodness. He will sell a great deal at the price which will yield the required profit to those who can sell only much less.

This is only another way of saying that the capital which yields the least permanent return—the least profit for which farmers as a class will carry on agriculture—is that which determines the price of agricultural produce. This is the least which the farmer in the long run will sell for, and the most which he will be able to obtain   And this capital is that which pays the least rent.

In all countries where land is easily accessible to capital, that "least" rent is *no* rent, because land is taken into cultivation as soon as its cultivation will pay the usual profit, and because after it is in cultivation, more and more capital is expended upon it, so long as expenditure meets with the usual return. The production of valuable things on the surface of the ground is exactly like the extraction of valuable things from beneath that surface.   It is the worst mine which can in the long run be kept going, that in the long run determines the price of the produce ; the owner of the better mine does not sell his ore cheaper than his neighbour, because he can get that ore at less cost than his neighbour ; the best-circumstanced miner exacts as much as the worst-circumstanced miner is able to obtain.   And the "worst-circumstanced" mine pays no royalty to the owner at all ; it only pays a bare profit on the capital.

Adam Smith's idea, therefore, that in ordinary circumstances the rent of land entered as an element into the price of agricultural produce, though a very natural idea, was a complete mistake, because he could not have told what rent he meant—the rent of best, or middling, or bad land—and because much capital employed in agriculture yields only the ordinary profit on capital, and therefore pays no rent at all.   The mode of estimating "cost of production," given by Adam Smith. in this case was most imperfect, because one of its terms was undetermined, a variable which might be anything, and often is nothing.

This opinion of Adam Smith's as to the rent of land is closely connected with a peculiar opinion of his as to agriculture. He held that it was the most profitable employment to which the capital and industry of a country could be directed. This opinion, like many of his others, was a modification of that which he had learned in France. The *économistes* in Paris at that time held that agriculture was the only profitable occupation of labour and capital. And it would take many pages to give an account in the least comprehensible, of the elaborate reasoning by which they had persuaded themselves of this ridiculous result. Adam Smith, of course, rejected it; his strong sense particularly revolted from that kind of argumentative absurdity. But he was nevertheless influenced by it. Though he did not hold agriculture to be the only source of profit, he held that it was a particularly prolific one. "It keeps three people," he would have said, "the landlord, the capitalist farmer, and the labourer; manufacturers and trade keep only two, the labourer and capitalist; clearly therefore agriculture has the advantage." He assigned at length what he thought was the philosophical reason. "The labourers and labouring cattle, therefore, employed in agriculture, not only occasion, like the workmen in manufactures, the reproduction of a value equal to their own consumption, or to the capital which employs them, together with its owner's profits; but of a much

greater value. Over and above the capital of the
farmer and all its profits, they regularly occasion the
reproduction of the rent of the landlord. This rent
may be considered as the produce of those powers
of nature, the use of which the landlord lends to the
farmer. It is greater or smaller according to the
supposed extent of those powers, or, in other words,
according to the supposed natural or improved
fertility of the land. It is the work of nature which
remains after deducting or compensating everything
which can be regarded as the work of man. It is seldom less than a fourth, and frequently more than a
third, of the whole produce. No equal quantity of productive labour employed in manufactures can ever
occasion so great a reproduction. In them nature
does nothing; man does all; and the reproduction
must always be in proportion to the strength of the
agents that occasion it. The capital employed in
agriculture, therefore, not only puts into motion a
greater quantity of productive labour than any equal
capital employed in manufactures, but, in proportion
too to the quantity of productive labour which it
employs, it adds a much greater value to the annual
produce of the land and labour of the country, to the
real wealth and revenue of its inhabitants. Of all
the ways in which a capital can be employed, it is
by far the most advantageous to the society."

Probably few passages in so eminent a writer on
the subject for which he is eminent, contain so much
curious falsehood. If nature does nothing in manufactures, in what is it that it does anything?
"Manufactures" are but applications of natural

forces, just as agriculture is another application. And the reasoning assumes that the natural causes which produce *dear* things are more beneficial to mankind than those which produce *cheap* things, though had Adam Smith seen that he was making such an assumption he would have been the first to reject it. The causes which produce dear things are not necessarily more beneficial than those which produce cheap ones; they are only less plentiful. A diamond mine is not more useful to the State than a coal mine; probably in the strictest sense of the word not so useful. The fact that a particular occupation keeps three classes of men, while other occupations only keep two, only shows that there is a special difficulty in getting into that occupation, and a special scarcity in its opportunities; it proves nothing as to the degree of good which it does for the public. And Adam Smith's conclusion is encumbered with the further absurdity that agriculture in new colonies does not create rent, and does not keep three people, though of course it is just as good for the public there as in old countries.

Although, therefore, Adam Smith had the merit of teaching the world that the exchangeable value of commodities is proportioned to the cost of their production, his analysis of that cost was so very defective as to throw that part of Political Economy into great confusion for many years, and as quite to prevent his teaching being used as an authority upon it now.

The causes which regulate the value of securities, whether debts or shares, Adam Smith did not

attempt to investigate at all; and it was not to be
expected that he should do so, for such things were
in his day a very unimportant part of wealth, compared with that which they are now.   And if, as we
have seen, Adam Smith's conception of "average"
value, and of the causes producing it, was then imperfect, his idea of monetary or market value was
much worse.   He says: "The actual price at which
any commodity is commonly sold is called its market
price.   It may either be above, or below, or exactly
the same with its natural price.   The market price
of every particular commodity is regulated by the
proportion between the quantity which is actually
brought to market, *and the demand of those who are
willing to pay the natural price of the commodity,* or the
whole value of the rent, labour, and profit, which
must be paid in order to bring it thither.   Such
people may be called the effectual demanders, and
their demand the effectual demand; since it may be
sufficient to effectuate the bringing of the commodity
to market.   It is different from the absolute demand.
A very poor man may be said in some sense to have
a demand for a coach and six; he might like to have
it; but his demand is not an effectual demand, as
the commodity can never be brought to market in
order to satisfy it."

But the actual price at which a thing is sold is
determined not solely by the demands of those who
are willing to pay the average price of the commodity,
but by everybody's demand who bids for it.   It is, as
we have seen, an exchange determined by the quantity of the commodity in the market and the desires

of its holders, as compared with the quantity of money in that market and the desires of its holders ; it is a case of barter determined by relative quantities and relative feelings. And the phrase " effectual demand," if defined to mean the demand of those willing to pay cost price, is misleading, because the money offered by those willing to pay cost price is not sufficient to be effectual when articles are particularly in demand, and therefore sell for more than it cost to make them, and is more than sufficient to be effectual when the demand for articles is particularly slack, and when therefore they sell for less than it cost to make them. The whole idea is confused.

In other passages, Adam Smith takes a view far better than in this. But this is the place where he ought to have taken the best, for it is the guiding paragraph of his special disquisition upon the subject. And his being not so good upon it here as elsewhere shows that his elementary conception was defective in definiteness. And nothing is more natural than that it should be so. Perhaps, as I have said before, Adam Smith's mind was by nature rather disinclined to an anxious accuracy in abstract ideas, and a century of critics on these facts and these times have sharpened our perception since he wrote on them. We must not expect from him the use of modern " words of precision," any more than we should find fault with a marksman of his generation for not using a rifle. Neither such " arms of precision," nor such " words of precision," then existed. And there was then little encouragement

to think out the subject. Adam Smith evidently
hurries over the abstract part of it, because he thinks
his readers will not attend to it. Even now a writer,
who wishes to be read beyond a very narrow circle,
must be careful not to be too elaborate. And in the
last century the case was certainly far worse. Many
great writers—Montesquieu and Hume especially—
would have written far more instructively, and as we
should now think, far better, if they could have relied
on any careful attention from their readers. They
evidently thought that their writings would be
principally read by persons who would cease to read
as soon as they became dull. Now-a-days the
diffusion of physical science—even of popular physical science—has partly taught us that much truth is
dull and complex, and that the most interesting
parts of truth can only be understood by those who
have mastered that dull and complex part. But
even now we do not remember this half enough.

After these specimens, it would evidently be tedious
to criticise *The Wealth of Nations* as if it were a
treatise of modern Political Economy. We have
given some account of what would be its answer to
the first question of that science, " What makes all
things exchange for more or less of other things ? "
And we see from it what the answer to other similar
questions would be like. Nothing could be more
unjust to a great writer than to judge of him by a
standard which he did not expect, and to blame his
best book for not being what he never thought of
making it, especially when, except for him, we should
never have imagined the standard, or conceived the

possibility of the book being that which we now blame it for not being. We might as well expect that the first cultivators of a country should make the best permanent road, as that the first pro-pounders of great conceptions should shape them into the finished form most useful to posterity.

The ways really to appreciate Adam Smith are two. First,—You should form a clear notion of the state of the received Political Economy of the world at the time he wrote. The last treatise on the sub-ject published in England before *The Wealth of Nations*, was *The Principles of Political Economy*, by Sir James Steuart. The author was a man of culture and travel, acquainted with a great variety of eco-nomic facts, and conversant with what had been written before upon the subject. He was a man of considerable natural ability, respected and consulted in his time, and his book is still worth looking over, for it contains many facts and reasonings which are curious. And this is the sort of thing he writes. Much foreign trade he considers mischievous. He propounds a plan—a foreign trade that is really desirable for a nation founded on the three following " easy principles ".

" The first,—That in a country entirely taken up with the object of foreign trade, no competition should be allowed to come from abroad for articles of the first necessity, and principally for food, so as to raise prices beyond a certain standard.

" The second,—That no domestic competition should be encouraged upon articles of superfluity, so as to raise prices beyond a certain standard.

" The third,—That when these standards cannot be preserved, and that, from natural causes, prices get above them, public money must be thrown into the scale to bring prices to the level of those of exportation.

" The greater the extent of foreign trade in any nation is, the lower these standards *must* be kept; the less the extent of it is, the higher they may be allowed to rise." [1]

And taking the subject more practically, he says : " It is a general maxim to discourage the importation of work, and to encourage the exportation of it," and upon that footing he asks and discusses : " What is the proper method to put a stop to a foreign trade in manufactures when the balance of it turns against a nation ? " This is the kind of authoritative doctrine which ruled in Adam Smith's time, and from which he delivered us.

The second way is to take up Adam Smith himself and read him. There are scarcely five consecutive pages in *The Wealth of Nations*, which do not contain some sound and solid observation important in practice and replete with common-sense. The most experienced men of business would have been proud of such a fund of just maxims fresh from the life, and it is wonderful that they should have occurred to an absent student, apparently buried in books and busy with abstractions. Most of such students, so far from being able to make such remarks, would not comprehend their value—would

[1] *Principles of Political Economy*, by Sir James Steuart, vol. i., p. 358.

acknowledge that they could not see much in them, if they were elaborately explained to them. Adam Smith himself probably did not know their exceeding merit, and preferred more learned parts of his writings, which are now obsolete, and more refined parts, which are now seen to have little value. Lord Bacon says of some one that he was "like Saul, who went in search of his father's asses and found a kingdom"; and this is exactly what happened to Adam Smith. He was engaged in a scheme of vast research, far surpassing the means at his disposal, and too good for any single man. In the course of that great pursuit, and as a small part of it, he came upon the "Wealth of Nations," for dealing with which his powers and his opportunities peculiarly fitted him, and on that he wrote a book, which has itself deeply influenced thought and policy, and which has been the beginning of a new science. He has obtained great fame, though it was not that fame which was the dream of his life, for—

> What was before us we know not,
> And we know not what shall succeed.[1]

[1] Matthew Arnold.

MALTHUS.

THE next great advance in Political Economy was made almost in as unlikely a manner. In the middle of the last century there lived in the south of England a certain Mr. David Malthus, who was a friend and correspondent of Rousseau, and one of his executors. This gentleman had adopted all Rousseau's ideas of the perfectibility of man, and of the speed with which he would improve if he were only left to himself, and set free from the chains of ancient custom The air of that time was full of such ideas, an. many otherwise quiet and rational persons were excited and enthusiastic about them. Mr. David Malthus had a clever son, Robert, whom he educated with great care, and to whom, doubtless, in season and out of season, he communicated his favourite ideas. At any rate, Robert grew up with a proper antipathy to them. The instinctive reaction of child against parent, which more than almost anything keeps men moving, and prevents " one good custom " from " corrupting the world," has seldom had a better example. " Train up a child in the way he should go," a cynic has observed, " and then you may feel safe that he will not walk in it." Let a child hear much from infancy of nice dreams and pleasing visions, and to the best of your ability you will have prepared him for prosaic carefulness and a dismal rationalism.

The *Essay on Population*, says Mr. Malthus, " which I published in 1798, was suggested, as is stated in the preface, by a paper in Mr. Godwin's *Enquirer;* " and there is a curious story about it. Mr. Godwin was a disciple of Rousseau, and had drawn up a plan of village perfection, in which " every rood was to maintain " its man, and in which mankind were to be happy and at ease, without the annoying restraints of property and marriage. Such " Elysiums " have been sketched in all ages, and here is nothing remarkable about them ; but Mr. Malthus's reply was very remarkable. " You may," he said, " imagine this perfect picture for a little while, but it will not last. It cannot last. Nature is against it. She has a principle—that of population—which is sure to destroy it. Mankind always, by her arrangements, increase as fast as they can ; misery checks their increase, and vice checks it, but nothing else. A perfectly happy and virtuous community, by physical law, is constrained to increase very rapidly ; if you look into the fact you will find that it will double every twenty-five years, but there can be no similar increase in their food. The best lands are taken up first, then the next best, then the inferior, at last the worst ; at each stage the amount of food produced is less than before. By nature human food increases in a slow arithmetical ratio ; man himself increases in a quick geometrical ratio, unless want and vice stop him, so that if you make him happy in a village community for a moment, he will soon multiply so that he shall cease to be happy ; there is nothing to stop him ; he will ere long reach the inevitable limit where want and wickedness begin to keep him down."

The world rather eagerly read his doctrine, for the reaction against dreams and visions was strong in many minds. The event of the French Revolution had upset all calculation, broken up all pleasing visions, and disheartened half, or, indeed, much more than half, mankind. Mr. Malthus was as much the mouthpiece of his generation in exposing Utopias, as his father had been in accepting them. The *Essay on Population*, in its first edition, was read with eager avidity, and its doctrines seem to have been much believed.

Still, when examined, the tenets seemed startling, and what made them even more surprising was that their propounder, Mr. Malthus, was a clergyman. People objected, " Can this really be so ? Is it consistent with religion ? Can we believe that inevitably man is yoked to sin and misery ? That even if you make him good, and if goodness makes him happy, the structure of earth and nature is such as inevitably in a few years to make him miserable again ? How is this possible under a benevolent Creator ? How can it be made to accord with revelation ? " Such objections were difficult to answer, especially as Mr. Malthus was a simple candid man, and they seem to have had much effect in changing his views. At least, in the preface to the second edition, he tells us : " Throughout the whole of the present work, I have so far differed from the former, as to suppose the action of another check to population, which does not come under the head either of vice or misery ".

This is the celebrated principle of "self-restraint, moral or prudential". And he goes on to say that he has endeavoured to soften some of the harshest conclusions of the first essay. But he does not seem to see that he has cut away the ground of his whole argument. If there be this principle of virtuous self-restraint, he no longer answers Godwin; he no longer destroys the dreams of perfectibility. If it be possible for a perfectly virtuous community to limit their numbers, they will perform that duty just as they perform all others; there is no infallible principle that will break up the village community; it can adjust its numbers to its food, and may last for ever. In its first form the *Essay on Population* was conclusive as an argument, only it was based on untrue facts; in its second form it was based on true facts, but it was inconclusive as an argument.

From this unlucky beginning the established doctrine in Political Economy of "Population" is to be dated. And as was not unnatural, so odd a commencement was unfavourable to its comprehension. From the mode in which he first regarded the subject, it was natural that Mr. Malthus should think more of the painful aspects of the subject than of the opposite ones. At first there were no cheerful aspects; the doctrine was an apparatus for destroying cheerfulness; in its second and truer form it is far less painful, though like most great truths about the world (especially economic ones, which have so much to do with labour and toil), it has its painful side. But Mr. Malthus first put the painful side alone forward, fixed the public mind upon it, and for many years it could see no other.

There is much in the theory of population which it would require a large book to discuss, and I am far from pretending that I could write that book. Many most difficult questions of morals, and many others of physiology, must be treated of, and it is especially hard to discuss such questions *virginibus puerisque*, as almost all questions are now discussed. Some parts of it could scarcely be managed, except under the decent veil of a dead language. The conditions of marriage form only part of that subject, and a great deal would have to be written on that part in its relations to the actual past, and to the possible future. But what is necessary for abstract Political Economy is much easier. As has been previously explained, the peculiarity of this science is that it abstracts, that is, it seizes upon and alone considers the principal peculiarities of existing man as we find him in the principal commercial nations. It does not profess to be accurately complete as to those nations, even as they are now, still less as they once were, or as they may hereafter be ; and still less again does it pretend to be true of other nations, in ages of a different character, cast in a different mould, and occupied with different ideas. Human nature is so various that we cannot treat of it at once briefly and fully; we can only reason on short propositions, and, therefore, we must cut the subject up into distinct portions, each of which can be conceived of by itself and heard out by itself And no part of human nature is more infinite

than the relation between the sexes and its consequences.

Mr. Malthus had no idea of looking at the subject
in this way. He thought he was dealing with all
nations and all ages. In its original form the
Essay propounded a universal principle, destruc-
tive of golden visions; in its later forms he deals,
first, with principles of population in the most bar-
barous ages, and then with them in every variety
of society which he knew of—nomad or stationary,
commercial or agricultural; and there is much in
his discussion of the savage society, which is still
worth reading, and which was much before his time.
His mind was by nature indisposed for, and unfit for,
abstractions; indeed, if I may say so with reverence,
he always seems to me but a poor hand at a dry
argument. Like Adam Smith, he had no idea that
he was founding an abstract science ; he thought he
was dealing wholly with the concrete world, but it
so happened that his idea of the concrete world
coincided with the most convenient abstraction
that can be made from it, and so he became,
in spite of himself, the founder of an abstract
science.

The assumed laws of population in abstract Political Economy are these :—

First,—That population would soon outstrip the
means of feeding it, if it were not kept down by vice,
misery, or self-restraint.

Secondly,—That in a state of society where self-
restraint does not act at all, or only acts so little
that we need not think of it, population will augment

till the poorest class of the community have only just enough to support life.

Thirdly,—That in a community where self-restraint acts effectually, each class of the community will augment till it reaches the point at which it begins to exercise that restraint.

In the second case (which was all that Malthus thought of in his first edition), the population increases till it reaches a physical minimum of subsistence—one that is set by natural causes; in the other it increases till it reaches a moral minimum of subsistence—that is, one set by human choice. And it follows that in improving communities this moral minimum is commonly rising, for in most communities more self-restraint of this sort is desirable, and as people improve they mostly are more inclined to exercise it. The physical minimum must be a fixed minimum; the moral may be, and ordinarily is, a moving minimum. A Political Economist does not imagine (as I have previously explained) that vice, misery, and self-restraint are the only causes which affect the rate of increase of population. He well knows that many others act on it. All he says is, that in the principal commercial communities of the world these causes are now in most powerful operation, though they are retarded or helped by others, in a word, that these selected causes will in such communities produce the specified results, in more or less time, though there are other causes which aid in settling how long or how short that time is to be.

For example, it might well be (though I do not

know that it has been proved) that some races of men from inherent organisation tend to augment faster than other races. The causes which divide men into races are so many, so hidden, and produce so many effects, that it would not be strange if they had this effect among others. Perhaps there would be more *a priori* likelihood that they would have such an effect as this than that they would produce some actual effects which are quite certain. There is much evidence that different climates affect differently the sexual desires ; some aggravating them and some calming them. And it would seem likely that those races which had in this respect for ages been exposed to intensifying influences, would augment more rapidly than those which had been exposed to mitigating ones. Our knowledge of race-making causes is still most imperfect, and we can never trace race effects separately ; they are always combined with the effects of many other causes. In this case the confusion is peculiarly complex, for rules of morality—arising in unknown circumstances, and inherited for untold ages—so retard or quicken the growth of population that it is impossible to isolate the purely physiological phenomenon. Still the principles above laid down afford all possible room for it ; they will have their usual action, though morality will have a concurrent action.

Again, we may quite believe that the nervous conditions which luxury engenders are less favourable to the prolificness of population than simpler conditions. On this point, and on this point only, of the theory of population—Adam Smith had re-

markable and sound views. "A half-starved Highland woman," he tells us, "frequently bears more
than twenty children, while a pampered fine lady is
often incapable of bearing any, and is generally
exhausted by two or three. Barrenness, so frequent
among women of fashion, is very rare among those
of inferior station." Probably of all causes which
regulate the pace of population, the nervous state of
the woman is the most important, and it seems to
have a kind of cyclical course as society advances.
There is much reason to think that in the earliest
state in which we know men to have lived—the state
of the old slave age and the present savages—the
hard labour and insufficient food of the women tend
very much to keep down the increase of numbers.
At a later period the improvement of food, better
shelter, diminution of work during pregnancy, bring
the bearing power of women up to its maximum.
The Highland woman of Adam Smith probably was
able to bring into the world as many children, and,
physically at least, as strong children, as any one
who ever lived. After that, not only the luxury of
which he speaks, but education and the habit of
using the mind, tend almost certainly to diminish
the producing power. There is only a certain
quantity of force in the female frame, and if that
force is invested, so to say, in one way, it cannot be
used in another.

The same force acts, no doubt, on man, but probably differently. The use of the mind in some ways
certainly does not have much, if any, effect on the
power of increasing the race. The English judges

whose children Mr. Galton counted, showed very considerable capacity of this sort, and they worked in their way as hard as many people ever have or will. But for the most part they do their work with a joyous swing and impetus which show that it does not tell upon the nerves. But anxiety, as has been said, does so tell, and we have seen that there is reason to believe that it much tends to slacken the growth of population; and, probably, any of the higher exercises of the mind, which cause, as they all do, obscure and subtle pain, have a similar effect. But these are problems for the future. No one can say that they are solved as yet; indeed, we are only beginning to try to solve them. Some have been sanguine enough to fancy that the accumulation of them may in distant ages make a stationary state possible, and make it pleasant. But with this Political Economy has nothing to do. It deals with men here and now; it takes certain parts of their nature which are indisputable, and which are important, and considers how these would operate by themselves. Questions as to the ultimate effects of other agencies, physiological or mental, it leaves to other sciences and to futurity.

In the same way, then, Political Economy cannot by itself pretend to solve the many new problems which the sanitary condition of great cities suggests in this age of them. There can be little doubt that these great accumulations of human beings have at least three effects. First, Mr. Galton holds that they diminish in some unknown degree the number of births, "Again, there is a constant tendency of the best men in the country to settle in the great cities, where marriages are less prolific and children are less likely to live. Owing to these several causes, there is a steady check in an old civilisation upon the fertility of the abler classes ; the improvident and unambitious are those who chiefly keep up the breed. So the race gradually deteriorates, becoming in each successive generation less fitted for a high civilisation, although it retains the external appearances of one, until the time comes when the whole political and social fabric caves in, and a greater or less relapse to barbarism takes place, during the reign of which the race is perhaps able to recover its tone." And these consequences seem to Mr. Galton purely evil. But they do not seem so to me. No doubt it is an evil that the accumulation of men in cities weakens the frame, and that they have not the same energy or health as those in the country. Every one must regret this decline of power. But when power has declined in a certain race, it is better that that race should not increase as fast as others. We had better breed from hardy than from weakened speci-mens. The diminished growth of urban populations seems to be Nature's remedy for the diminution in their strength. Secondly, great towns indisputably encourage drunkenness. The bad state of the atmo-sphere there certainly inclines men more to drink than the better air of the country. And this is, no doubt, a great evil. But we may doubt if it is an evil without compensation. The persons most in-clined to drunkenness are generally persons of some nervous taint or weakness which they often inherited themselves, and which they might not improbably transmit to their children. I do not, of course, mean that this inherent weakness is irresistible. No doubt the mass of these people can, at first at least, help drinking very well. The heritable taint amounts only to an increased liability to this temptation. But this is quite reason enough to wish that it should not be inherited. Great cities seem to have this special function in the world, that they bring out this taint in the worst specimens. Not only do such persons suffer as usual from the general decline in the multiplying power of city populations, but they also suffer in a way peculiar to themselves. One of the effects of a drunken habit is to diminish this kind of power, as well as, and perhaps more than, most others. Thirdly, great cities collect together a great criminal population, and make them sterile ; and so far as crime is connected with a low type of nervous organisation, as it is very often, this sterility is a great gain. Society gets rid of these over-tempted persons, whose peculiar defects are a danger to others as well as to themselves. Great cities must always be in their worst aspects painful spectacles, but this painfulness is somewhat relieved when we see that we can regard them as a huge cleansing machinery, which, no doubt, shows us a great deal that is detestable, but also takes away much of it, and prevents more coming, not only in that place but in others.

Nor has Political Economy any concern with the other purging means, which in a subtle way Nature seems to use all through civilised society. It is said

that man is the only animal of whose breed no
care is taken. But Nature has not forgotten to take
much care of it. Every one who watches society must
have seen many instances in which defective families have died out, because they were defective. The
men being weak failed to earn their living, and,
therefore, could not marry, and the girls wanting
from the same cause life and vigour did not find
husbands, and so the race died away. And this
cause works not only in families weak as a whole,
but in the weak members of strong families. All
through society there is a constant tendency in civilised life to slacken the pace of population by weed-
ing away those weaker and less valuable.

There seem to be curious processes of Nature also
at the other end of the scale of cultivation. The
process by which so many savage races die out before
civilised man, is certainly not as yet completely
explained. Hard work, which civilised man brings,
and which most savages cannot bear, accounts for
some of it; alcohol, "the fire-water," as savages
call it, accounts for more. But there seems to be a
residue still unexplained. The most plausible theory
says that this is due to two causes; and first, to the
inability of savage nations to bear the diseases to
which the hardened frame of civilised men is inured.
For ages, in the contested parts of the world which
civilised man inhabits, the stronger race has conquered and supplanted the weaker, and the result
is a strong animal equal to many difficulties, and
able among other things to survive strong diseases.
But in the out-of-the-way places which savages in-

habit there has been no such incessant conflict, and in consequence there is no such strong animal. The weaker savage succumbs to diseases which the seasoned white man easily bears. Indeed, the way in which savages waste away before "alcohol" is but a case of this; they cannot bear, as white men can, the diseases which it generates. And the second cause which co-operates with this is a certain disheartened tendency of mind which somehow tells on the nerves and which is analogous to the way in which wild animals die out when caught and confined. A certain life and spirit seem as essential to keep men in good numbers as in good health.

Different kinds of food may, too, for ought we know, have an effect not yet understood on man's power to increase his numbers. The potato was at one time fancied—erroneously, probably—to contain a particular stimulus of this sort. But though this instance may have been a mistake, the conception is possible. We must not always say that the more nutritious food will tend universally to produce the more people, though, no doubt, it usually does so. It may even sometimes have a contrary effect; it may run to quality rather than to quantity; it may make fewer strong people, instead of more weak ones.

I set out these considerations at length because it is most important that there should be no disunion between Political Economy and Physiology, or between it and the more complex forms of social science. No Political Economist has the slightest reason to depreciate the causes which act on population of which his science takes no cognisance. On the contrary, he has the greatest reason for taking an interest in them. They supplement what he discusses; reality is composed of the influences treated of in his science, *plus* these influences, and of course he wishes to compare his work with fact.

We must be careful to see what these principles themselves mean, for they are often mistaken. Even apart from Physiology, they do not say that an increase in the comfort of a people necessarily tends to augment their numbers. It does so in two cases only. The first case is when the people are at the "physical minimum," with just enough to support life, and do not exercise self-restraint. Here the moment there is more food there will be more numbers. Such people will always multiply, just as the ryots in Bengal, in a somewhat similar state of things, are multiplying. The second case is when the people are at the "moral minimum," with just what will support the existing numbers in the sort of life they think proper—be it high or low—such numbers being kept down by self-restraint, and when the people do not change their standard. Then, undoubtedly, more comfort will be turned into more children, and in a little while the new state of things will produce no more comfort to each person than the old one—only there will be more persons to enjoy it. But there is no sort of necessity in this; as has been explained, the "moral minimum" is very movable; the people may change their standard, and in that case more comfort will not produce more persons. There will only be as many as there would have been before, and the

average of these will have a better life. Whether a
people take one course or the other, will depend on
this sort of change, and on its relation to the sort of
civilisation enjoyed by the people. I doubt if any
general formula can be found for it. Some writers
have said that a great sudden change which elevates
a whole generation, is more likely to raise the
population standard than a series of successive small
changes. But as far as I can judge, more depends
on the previous preparation of the people than on its
absolute amount ; a really thrifty people used to self-
denial will profit exceedingly by a series of small
improvements ; they will not "run to numbers,"
they will augment in happiness. And an easy-going
enjoying nation will mostly not be much the better
for any boon of plenty, however great or sudden ;
they will live at the same average, but the average
will not be raised.

Now that we see the extreme delicacy of the
assumptions as to population on which abstract
Political Economy is based, we shall not be surprised
at finding that Mr. Malthus did not apprehend them
as they really are. As I have said, he did not in the
least know that he was aiding in the foundation of
an abstract science. He thought that he was dealing with real men and that the principles which he
expounded were all those which affected his subject.
Indeed, the best part of his book is an account,
which must have cost great labour at that time, of
the rate at which population had augmented, and
was augmenting, in various countries, and the
causes which influenced that rate. And the best

part of this is that which relates to the savage
state, for even now when that state has been so
accurately studied, it is worth while to glance over
what Malthus wrote on it, more than fifty years ago.
That his analysis of population causes in other
countries should be most incomplete was a matter
of course; even now we are in the dark on much
of this subject.   But how incomplete it was will
sufficiently appear from a single fact.   Though he
treats elaborately of Norway and of Switzerland,
he has no idea that peasant properties have a tendency to check population   He discusses the subject
as if there were no difference in this respect between
a people which owns the soil and one which lives by
wages.   And therefore many of the disquisitions in
which he indulges are wholly thrown away.

And Mr. Malthus, as was natural, never cleared
his mind entirely of the dismal theory with which he
began.   Scarcely any man who has evolved a striking
and original conception of a subject ever gets rid of
it.   Long after he himself fancies that he has cleared
his mind of it, every one else sees that it haunts him
still.   Mr. Malthus was peculiarly little likely to get
rid of his errors.   He had published his original
theory, had made a name by publishing it, and he
never admitted even to himself how complete a
change the foundation of his ideas had undergone.
A theory of population which does not include self-
restraint, like his first, and one which essentially
depends on it, like his second, differ in their essence,
and therefore differ in their main consequences.
From a theory of population which does not include

a prudential check, it follows that plenty cannot last, and that men will always multiply down to misery. But such a theory with a prudential check, has no such consequence. And for many years it was a misfortune to the subject that the original propounder of what were then the best views of it, had connected those views with a mischievous exaggeration, leading straight to lamentable results.

To most other parts of Political Economy Mr. Malthus added very little. And on some he supported errors which were even then becoming antiquated. He was a strenuous advocate of "Protection to Agriculture," and believed that the supply of all commodities might exceed the demand, which is as much as to say that there is too much of everything. The truth is, that Mr. Malthus had not the practical sagacity necessary for the treatment of Political Economy in a concrete way, or the mastery of abstract ideas necessary to deal with it in what we should now call a scientific way. He tried a bad mixture of both. There is a mist of speculation over his facts, and a vapour of fact over his ideas.

On one important point Mr. Malthus was, however, in advance of his time. He was one of several writers who, at the same time, discovered the true theory of rent. That theory lay, indeed, close to his ideas on population. Its essence (as we have seen) is, that the rent of land arises from the scarcity of good land. Mr. Malthus could not help seeing that Adam Smith (and the French *économistes*) were wrong in imputing rent to some pre-eminent merit in the

land.   He saw that it came from a special fact
concerning land, *viz.*, that so little of it is first-rate
both in situation and in quality ; that most is either
not the best, or not in the best place, else there
would be no rent of land any more than of air.   This
truth seems so plain that one can scarcely conceive
how it should ever not have been seen.   But
certainly it was not seen till modern economists
pointed it out.   And, then, as so often happens, it
was on many people's lips almost at once.   The
fact was so unmistakably plain that several persons
could not help seeing it the moment they began to
search for it.   Of these, Mr. Malthus was one, but
not the best.   As we shall see, a much keener
intellect than his far more fully examined all its
consequences.

There is nothing in Mr. Malthus's life which is
worth mentioning, or which illustrated his doctrines.
He was an estimable gentleman, and clerical professor ; a " mild pottering person," I think Carlyle
would have called him.   Neither his occupation nor
his turn of mind particularly fitted him to write on
money matters.   He was not a man of business, nor
had he, like Paley, and similar clergymen, a hard-
headed liking for, and an innate insight into, the theory
of business.   He was a sensible man educated in the
midst of illusions ; he felt a reaction against them,
and devoted the vigour of his youth to disprove and
dispel them.   And he made many sensible and acute
remarks on kindred topics.   But he has been among
the luckiest of authors, for he has connected his
name with the foundation of a lasting science which

he did not plan, and would by no means have agreed in.

This celebrity may seem over-fortunate, but it is explained by the circumstances of the time. The age in which he wrote was as much against the Godwinian illusions as Mr. Malthus could be. He and his father were but an instance of a general contrast between successive generations. The generation before 1789 was full of hope, and delighted with happy schemes; that after it was terrified by the French Revolution, insensible to hope and ready for despair. To this change of sentiment Mr. Malthus effectually ministered, and beneath this want of the surface there was one much more real need, to which he was of use also. An immense tide of sentiment favoured the growth of population, no matter what the circumstances and what its means of subsistence. Mr. Pitt, who was the most instructed statesman of the time on economic subjects said that " the man who had a large family was 'a benefactor to his country' ". And the old English Poor Law was simply a subsidy to the increase of paupers. Against such notions and such practices Mr. Malthus's views were a most admirable reaction. If there had been no such movement our agricultural districts would by this time have been a pauper warren. That his views were exaggerated, though a subsequent misfortune, was an immediate advantage. He advertised his notions and fixed them among the men who understood a simple and striking exaggeration far more easily than a full and accurate truth. He created an entirely new feeling on his subject.

" If we look," says Mr. Carlyle, " at the old Poor Law, we shall find it to have become still more insupportable, demanding, if England was not destined for anarchy, to be done away with." " To create men filled with a theory " that it ought to be done away with " was the one thing needful " ; " nature had no readier way of getting it done away with ". To this Mr. Malthus most essentially contributed. It was he who, more than any one else, " filled " men with that theory.

RICARDO.

THE true founder of abstract Political Economy is Ricardo. And yet in seeming there was no one less likely to be the founder. He was a practical man of business, who had little education, who was for much of his life closely occupied in a singularly absorbing trade, and who made a fortune in that trade. Just as no one would have expected from Adam Smith, the bookish student, the practical sagacity with which every page of *The Wealth of Nations* overflows, so no one would have expected from Ricardo, who made a large fortune, the foundation of a science of abstractions. Every one would, on the contrary, have imagined that Adam Smith would have been eminent in the abstractions among which his closet-life would seem to have been spent, and that Ricardo would have been eminent in the rough and rude sense which makes money. But, in fact, Ricardo arrives at his best conclusions by the most delicate and often difficult reasoning, and Adam Smith, as we have seen, at his by an easy and homely sagacity.

There is much in this, as in all such cases, which now is, and probably will always remain, inexplicable; for the most obscure and subtle of causes are those which fix inherited genius. But, just as in Adam Smith's case, a more exact survey of the circumstances tends to diminish our surprise. The trade in which Ricardo spent his life, and in which he was so successful, is of all trades the most abstract. Perhaps some people may smile when they hear that his money was made on the Stock Exchange, which they believe to be a scene of gambling. But there is no place where the calculations are so fine, or where they are employed on *data* so impalpable and so little "immersed in matter". There is a story that some dealer made very many thousand pounds by continued dealings in the shares of some railway, and then on a sudden asked where that railway was. The whole thing had been a series of algebraic quantities to him, which called up no picture, but which affected a profit and loss account. In most kinds of business there is an appeal of some sort to the senses; there are goods in ships or machines; even in banking there is much physical money to be counted. But the Stock Exchange deals in the "debts," that is the "promises," of nations, and in the "shares" of undertakings whose value depends on certain future dividends—that is, on certain expectations—and what those expectations are to be, is a matter of nice calculation from the past. These imponderable elements of trade cannot be seen or handled, and the dealing with them trains the mind to a refinement analogous to that of the metaphysician. The ordinary human mind finds a great rest in fixing itself on a concrete object, but neither the metaphysician nor the stock-jobber has any such means of repose. Both must make their minds ache by fixing them intently on what they can never see, and by working out all its important qualities and quantities. A stock-jobber loses money, and in the end is ruined, if he omits any, or miscalculates any. If any man of business is to turn abstract thinker, this is the one who should do so. Any careful reader of Ricardo, who knows anything of such matters, and who watches the anxious penetration with which he follows out rarefied minutiæ, will very often say to himself, " I see well why this man made a fortune on the Stock Exchange ".

For this trade Ricardo had the best of all preparations—the preparation of race. He was a Jew by descent (his father was one by religion), and for ages the Jews have shown a marked excellence in what may be called the " commerce of imperceptibles ". They have no particular superiority in the ordinary branches of trade; an Englishman is quite their equal in dealing with ordinary merchandise, in machine-making, or manufacturing. But the Jews excel on every Bourse in Europe; they—and Christian descendants of their blood—have a pre-eminence there wholly out of proportion to their numbers or even to their wealth. Some part of that pre-eminence is, no doubt, owing to their peculiar position as a race; for nearly two thousand years they have been a small nation diffused over a vast area; that diffusion has made them the money-lenders for most of the nations with whom they lived; and the exchange of money between country and country is a business of fine calculation, which prepared them for other fine calculations. This long experience has probably developed a natural aptitude, and it would be idle to distinguish what is due to the one in comparison with the other. The fact remains that the Jews have now an inborn facility in applying figures to pure money matters. They want, less than other nations, a visible commodity which they can imagine, if not touch; they follow with greater ease and greater nicety all the minute fractions on which this subtle commerce depends (a task which is a particular torture to most Englishmen), and they make money as the result. The writings of Ricardo are unique in literature, so far as I know, as a representative on paper of the special faculties by which the Jews have grown rich for ages. The works of Spinoza, and many others, have shown the power of the race in dealing with other kinds of abstraction; but I know none but Ricardo's which can awaken a book-student to a sense of the Jewish genius for the mathematics of money-dealing. His mastery over the abstractions of Political Economy is of a kind almost exactly identical.

The peculiar circumstances of his time also conducted Ricardo to the task for which his mind was most fit. He did not go to Political Economy—Political Economy, so to say, came to him. He lived in the "City" at a time when there was an incessant economic discussion there. He was born in 1772, and had been some years in business in 1797, the year of the celebrated "Bank restriction," which "restricted" the Bank of England from paying its notes in coin, and which established for the next twenty years in England an inconvertible paper currency. As to this—as to the nature of its effect, and even as to whether it had an effect,—there was an enormous amount of controversy. Ricardo could not have helped hearing of it, and after some years took an eager part in it. Probably, if he had not been led in this way to write pamphlets, he would never have written anything at all, or have got the habit of consecutive dealing with difficult topics, which is rarely gained without writing. He had only a common school education, and no special training in such things. But it is the nature of an inconvertible currency to throw the dealings between other countries and the country which has it, into confusion, and to change the price of all its securities. As Ricardo was a jobber on the English Stock Exchange for the whole time during which the notes of the Bank of England were inconvertible, his daily business must have constantly felt the effect.

Having been thus stimulated to write pamphlets on the one great economic subject of his day, Ricardo was naturally led to write them also on the other great one. At the close of the war the English Parliament was afraid that corn would be too cheap ; the war had made it dear, and probably when peace came it would cease to be dear. And therefore, in its wisdom, Parliament passed " Corn Laws " to keep it dear. And it would have been difficult for a keen arguer and clear thinker like Ricardo to abstain from proving that Parliament was wrong. And, accordingly, he wrote some essays which would be called " dry and difficult " now, but which were then read very extensively and had much influence.

Political Economy was, indeed, the favourite subject in England from about 1810 to 1840, and this to an extent which the present generation can scarcely comprehend. Indeed, old people are puzzled for an opposite reason; they can hardly understand the comparative disappearance of what was the principal topic in their youth. They mutter, with extreme surprise, "we hardly hear anything now about Political Economy; we used to hear of nothing so much". And the fundamental cause is the great improvement in the condition of the country. For the thirty years succeeding the peace of 1815 England was always uncomfortable. Trade was bad, employment scarce, and all our industry depressed, fluctuating, and out of heart. So great is the change of times, that what we now call bad trade would then have seemed very good trade, and what we now call good trade would have been too good to be thought of—would have been deemed an inconceivable Elysian and Utopian dream. So long as this misery and discomfort continued, there was a natural curiosity as to the remedy. Business being bad, there was a great interest in the "science of business," which ought to explain why it was thus bad, and might be able to show how it was to be made good. While the economic condition of countries is bad, men care for Political Economy, which may tell us how it is to be improved; when that condition is improved, Political Economy ceases to have the same popular interest, for it can no longer prescribe anything which helps the people's life. In no age of England, either before or since, could a practical man of business, like Ricardo, have had so many and such strong influences combining to lead him towards Political Economy, as in Ricardo's own time.

And there was at that time a philosophical fashion which was peculiarly adapted to make him think that the abstract mode of treating the subject which was most suitable to his genius was the right mode. It was the age of " philosophical Radicalism," a school of philosophy which held that the whole theory of Political Government could be deduced from a few simple axioms of human nature. It assumed certain maxims as to every one's interest, and as to every one always following his interest, and from thence deduced the universal superiority of one particular form of Government over all others. " Euclid " was its one type of scientific thought, and it believed that type to be, if not always, at least very often, attainable. From a short series of axioms and definitions it believed that a large part of human things, far more than is really possible, could be deduced. The most known to posterity of this school (and probably its founder) was Mr. Bentham, for the special value of his works on jurisprudence has caused his name to survive the general mode of political thinking which he was so powerful in introducing. But a member of the sect, almost equally influential in his own time, was Mr. James Mill, of whom his son has given us such a graphic picture in his biography. This austere dogmatist thought that the laws of Government and of human happiness might be evolved from some few principles, just as a Calvinistic theologian evolves a whole creed of human salvation from certain others. Mr. Grote, who belonged for the best years of his life to the sect, and whose writings and tone of mind were profoundly tinctured by its teaching, has left us a vivid description of Mr. James Mill, who seems to have influenced him far more than any one else. And an equally vivid picture may still be found in the reminiscences of a few old men, who still linger in London society, and who are fond of recalling the doctrines of their youth, though probably they now no longer believe them. James Mill must have pre-eminently possessed the Socratic gift of instantaneously exciting and permanently impressing the minds of those around him.

I do not know in what manner Ricardo and James Mill became acquainted, except that John Mill says it was through Bentham, who was a rich man, and, though a recluse, made for many years his house a sort of castle. John Mill tells us also that James Mill considered the friendship of Ricardo to have been the most valuable of his whole life. To a genius like Ricardo, with Ricardo's time and circumstances, the doctrines of James Mill must have come like fire to fuel; they must have stimulated the innate desire to deduce in systematic connection from the fewest possible principles, the truths which he had long been considering disconnectedly. If Ricardo had never seen James Mill he would probably have written many special pamphlets of great value on passing economic problems, but he would probably not have written *On the Principles of Political Economy and Taxation*, and thus founded an abstract science; it takes a great effort to breathe for long together the "thin air" of abstract reasoning.

It must be remembered that Ricardo was in no high sense an educated man. As far as we know he had not studied any science, and had no large notion of what science was; without encouragement from a better-trained mind he most likely would not have attempted any purely scientific effort. To the end of his days, indeed, he never comprehended what he was doing. He dealt with abstractions without knowing that they were such; he thoroughly believed that he was dealing with real things. He thought that he was considering actual human nature in its actual circumstances, when he was really considering a fictitious nature in fictitious circumstances. And James Mill, his instructor on general subjects, had on this point as little true knowledge as he had himself. James Mill, above all men, believed that you could work out the concrete world of human polity and wealth from a few first truths. He would have shuddered at our modern conception of Political Economy as a convenient series of deductions from assumed axioms which are never quite true, which in many times and countries would be utterly untrue, but which are sufficiently near to the principal conditions of the modern world to make it useful to consider them by themselves. At that time economists indulged in happy visions; they thought the attainment of truth far easier than we have since found it to be. They were engaged in a most valuable preliminary work, one which is essential to the conception of the phenomena of wealth in such an age as this, or in any age in which free industry has made much progress; but after this preliminary work is finished there is a long and tedious time to be spent in comparing the assumptions we have made in it with the facts which we see, and in adding the corrections which that comparison suggests; and only at the end of this dull task can we leave mere reasoning and come to life and practice.

Little is known of Ricardo's life, and of that little only one thing is worth mentioning in a sketch like this—that he went into Parliament. He had retired with a large fortune from business comparatively young, not much over forty, as far as I can make out, and the currency and other favourite economic subjects of his were so much under discussion in Parliament, that he was induced to enter it. At present an abstract philosopher, however wealthy, does not often enter Parliament; there is a most toilsome, and to him probably disagreeable, labour to be first undergone—the canvassing a popular constituency. But fifty years ago this was not essential. Ricardo entered Parliament for Portarlington, which is now the smallest borough in Ireland, or indeed, in the whole United Kingdom, and which was then a mere rotten or proprietary borough, and no doubt Ricardo bought his seat of the proprietor. He was well received in the House, and spoke with clearness and effect on his own subjects. He is said to have had in conversation a very happy power of lucid explanation, and he was able to use the same power in a continuous speech to an assembly. His wealth, no doubt, gave him a facility in acquiring respect. Parliament, like every other collection of Englishmen, is much more ready to trust a rich man about money than a poor one.

The most curious characteristic of Ricardo's political career was his zeal to abolish the means by which he entered Parliament; he was most anxious for a Parliamentary Reform much resembling in principle that of 1832. And in this he agreed with most of the sensible men of his time. The narrow-mindedness and the want of capacity with which the Tory party had governed the country since the peace, are now only known to us from history, and are not easily believed by those who have not carefully studied that history. As was the tree, so were its fruits; the Government seemed to be one which must hurt a country, and in fact the country was, if not very unhappy, at any rate most uncomfortable. The best cure seemed to be a change of rulers, by a large addition to the popular element in the Government. And, as we now know, this has been effectual. The country has been far happier under the new system than under the old, and the improvement has been greatly due to the change; we could not have had Free Trade before 1832, and it is Free Trade which more than any other single cause makes us so happy. The change in popular comfort has been greater than Ricardo or than any one of his generation could have imagined. But we have had to pay a good price for it, and one of the items in that price is the exclusion of philosophers from Parliament. Such a thinker as Ricardo, with the unflinching independence which characterised Ricardo, would be impossible in our recent Parliaments. No popular constituency would consent to elect such a man, nor would he consent to ask them.

Very little is now to be learnt of Ricardo's ordinary life. We know that he had a mind—

> keen, intense, and frugal,
> Apt for all affairs.

And we know little else. A well-authenticated tradition says that he was most apt and ready in the minutest numerical calculations. This might be gathered from his works, and, indeed, any one must be thus apt and ready who thrives on the Stock Exchange. A less authorised story says that he was a careful saver of small sums—"one of those people who would borrow a pamphlet, price sixpence, instead of buying it," notwithstanding that he was a rich man. We also know, as has been said, that he was very happy in orally explaining his doctrines, and they are by no means easy to explain in that way. He must have been most industrious, for he died at fifty-two ; and either the thinking which he did, or the fortune which he made, would be generally esteemed, even by laborious men, a sufficient result for so short a life.[1]

---

[1] [Mr. Bagehot had intended, as the reader will have seen, to give an estimate of J. S. Mill similar to those of Malthus and Ricardo. As he did not carry out this intention, I think it well to give some brief passages from a shorter paper on Mill, written on the occasion of his death, which contain Mr. Bagehot's general view of Mill's economic position. These will be found in Note B, at the end of the volume.—EDITOR.]

THE GROWTH OF CAPITAL.

THE conclusion that English Political Economy is
an analysis only of industrial societies which are to
a certain extent developed, will be strengthened by
a consideration of the doctrines which that Political
Economy teaches us as to one of the principal parts
of the subject—the theory of the growth of capital.
Our Political Economy does not recognise that
there is a vital distinction between the main mode
in which capital grows in such countries as England
now, and the mode in which it grew in all countries
at first.

The principal way in which capital increases in
England now, is by abstinence from enjoyment.
We receive our incomes in money, and either we
spend them on our enjoyments, in which case capital
is not increased, for our incomes are all gone and
no new productive thing is made, or we abstain
from enjoyment and put our money into trade ourselves, supposing that we are in trade, and supposing
that we are not in trade, lend it to those who are.
The productive part of wealth—the wealth which
creates other wealth—is augmented mainly by our
not enjoying our incomes.

But there is another mode of augmenting capital
of which Defoe gives us, perhaps, a more vivid
notion than we can get elsewhere. " I cannot say,'
says Robinson Crusoe, " that after this, for five

years, any extraordinary thing happened to me;
but I lived on in the same course, in the same pos-
ture and place just as before; the chief thing I was
employed in, besides my yearly labour of planting
my barley and rice, and curing my raisins, of both
which I always kept up just enough to have sufficient stock of the year's provisions beforehand; I
say, besides this yearly labour, and my daily labour
of going out with my gun, I had one labour to make
me a canoe, which at last I finished: so that by
digging a canal to it, six feet wide, and four feet
deep, I brought it into the creek, almost half a mile.
As for the first, that was so vastly big, as I made
it without considering beforehand, as I ought to do,
how I should be able to launch it; so never being
able to bring it to the water, or bring the water to
it, I was obliged to let it lie where it was, as a
memorandum to teach me to be wiser next time.
Indeed the next time though I could not get a tree
proper for it, and was in a place where I could not
get the water to it, at any less distance than, as I
have said, of near half a mile; yet as I saw it was
practicable at last, I never gave it over; and though
I was near two years about it, yet I never grudged
my labour, in hopes of having a boat to go off to
sea at last." But in this case there was evidently
no abstinence from enjoyment. Robinson Crusoe
had only the bare means of subsistence; he had no
pleasant things to give up; but he employed his
time and labour in making a vessel, a piece of
capital, if ever there was one.

Just similar is the practice of primitive societies.

When a savage in the stone age made a flint implement he relinquished no satisfaction. Having nothing else to do he made a tool, which has been the beginning of all other tools. " Mankind," says a recent wiiter,[1] " may have discovered how to manufacture earthen vessels in various ways. Sir John Lubbock points out that Captain Cook saw stones surrounded with a rim of clay in use among the Aleutians on Unalashka; but this might be an imitation of European vessels with which the islanders had already become acquainted through Russian sailors. The practice of the Australians on the Lower Murray River, of puddling holes in the earth with clay and cooking food in them, might perhaps have led an inventive mind to the manufacture of earthen vessels. But the process is better explained by the account of the French sailor Gonneville, who, in 1504, landed on a South Atlantic coast, probably in Brazil.[2] He describes certain wooden vessels in use among the natives (in whom D'Avezac fancies that he recognises Brazilian Carijo) enveloped in a coating of clay as a protection from the fire.[3] If by chance the wooden bowl separated itself from the covering of clay, an earthen vessel would remain. In examining the site of an old pottery manufactory of the Red Indians on the Cahokia, which falls into the Mississippi below St. Louis, Carl Rau discovered

[1] Oscar Peschel's *Races of Man and their Geographical Distribution*, page 168.

[2] Pierre Margry, *Les Navigations Françaises*, 1867.

[3] D'Avezac, *Voyage du Capitaine Gonneville*, 1869.

half-finished vessels, that is to say, baskets of rushes or willow, lined inside with clay."

These primitive potters had no luxuries to forego, and had no "income" to spend on luxuries. They simply had spare time and unused handiness, and with this they made the first pots, which were the beginning of all pots—the ancestors first of the tea kettle and then of the condensing engine.

In the same way there was no sacrifice of pleasure in the greatest source of early capital—the taming of animals; on the contrary, according to the most probable theory, there was a new pleasure in taming them which did not require the surrender of any old pleasure.

Mr. Galton has shown that in all probability the taming of animals began, not in the restraining of any impulses, but in the indulgence of some very simple ones.[1] "The domestication of animals," he tells us, "is one of the few relics of the past whence we may reasonably speculate on man's social condition in very ancient times. We know that the domestication of every important member of our existing stock originated in prehistoric ages, and, therefore, that our remote ancestors accomplished in a variety of cases, what we have been unable to effect in any single instance. The object of my paper is to discuss the character of ancient civilisation, as indicated by so great an achievement. Was there a golden age of advanced enlightenment?

---

[1] *Domestication of Animals*, by Francis Galton, F.R.S. Reprinted from the *Transactions of the Ethnological Society*, 1865, p. 1.

Have extraordinary geniuses arisen who severally taught their contemporaries to tame and domesticate the dog, the ox, the sheep, the hog, the fowl, the camel, the llama, the reindeer, and the rest? Or again, Is it possible that the ordinary habits of rude races, combined with the qualities of the animals in question, have sufficed to originate every instance of established domestication? The conclusion to which I have arrived, is entirely in favour of the last hypothesis. My arguments are contained in the following paper; but I will commence by stating their drift, lest the details I introduce should seem trifling or inconsequent. It will be this: All savages maintain *pet* animals, many tribes have *sacred* ones, and kings of ancient states have *imported* captive animals, on a vast scale, from their barbarian neighbours. I infer that every animal, of any pretensions, has been tamed over and over again, and has had numerous opportunities of becoming domesticated. But the cases are rare in which these opportunities can lead to any result. No animal is fitted for domestication unless it fulfils certain *stringent conditions*, which I will endeavour to state and to discuss. My conclusion is, that all domesticable animals of any note, have long ago fallen under the yoke of man. In short, that the animal creation has been pretty thoroughly, though half unconsciously, explored, by the every-day habits of rude races and simple civilisations."

And after enumerating the qualities which a tameable animal must possess, which are hardiness, fondness for man (which some animals now used have, while others have not), desire of comfort, easiness to tend, willingness to breed, and usefulness to the human race, he adds:[1] "The utility of the animals as a store of future food, is undoubtedly the most durable reason for maintaining them; but I think it was probably not so early a motive as the chief's *pleasure in possessing* them. That was the feeling under which the menageries, described above were established. Whatever the despot of savage tribes is pleased with, becomes invested with a sort of sacredness. His tame animals would be the care of all his people, who would become skilful herdsmen under the pressure of fear. It would be as much as their lives were worth if one of the creatures were injured through their neglect. I believe that the keeping of a herd of beasts, with the sole motive of using them as a reserve for food, or as a means of barter, is a late idea in the history of civilisation. It has now become established among the pastoral races of South Africa, owing to the traffickings of the cattle traders, but it was by no means prevalent in Damara-Land when I travelled there twelve years ago. I then was surprised to observe the considerations that induced the chiefs to take pleasure in their vast herds of cattle. They were valued for their stateliness and colour, far more than for their beef. They were as the deer of an English squire, or as the stud of a man who has many more horses than he can ride. An ox was almost a sacred beast in

[1] *Domestication of Animals*, by Francis Galton, F.R.S. Reprinted from the *Transactions of the Ethnological Society*, 1865, p. 14.

Damara-Land, not to be killed except on momentous occasions, and then as a sort of sacrificial feast, in which all bystanders shared. The payment of two oxen was hush-money for the life of a man. I was considerably embarrassed by finding that I had the greatest trouble in buying oxen for my own use, with the ordinary articles of barter. The possessors would hardly part with them for any remuneration; they would never sell their handsomest beasts." And he concludes: "I see no reason to suppose that the first domestication of any animal, except the elephant, implies a high civilisation among the people who established it. I cannot believe it to have been the result of a preconceived intention, followed by elaborate trials, to administer to the comfort of man. Neither can I think it arose from one successful effort made by an individual, who might thereby justly claim the title of benefactor to his race ; but, on the contrary, that a vast number of half-conscious attempts have been made throughout the course of ages, and that ultimately, by slow degrees, after many relapses, and continued selection, our several domestic breeds became firmly established."

This theory is one of the most valuable fruits of that contact of the most cultivated living minds with the least so—of men of science with savages, which is characteristic of this generation. And though its details may be modified, its essence seems certain, and it shows that this great form of early capital, the *live* form, did not begin with abstinence at all.

Even in such times as are described in the Book

of Genesis—the specially pastoral times—abstinence was not the main source of capital. When we are told that the flocks and herds of certain patriarchs "grew and multiplied exceedingly," those patriarchs were sacrificing nothing. They had enough to eat and to drink—the women of their household made their clothes—they had few other conscious wants, and still fewer means of supplying those which they had. The vast increase of animal power which helped on after-wealth so much, had probably its origin in the pride of the eye, in the love of the spectacle of wealth, as much as in anything. Abraham and Jacob were pleased to see "their cattle wax great and cover the whole land," and, therefore, they let them cover it. There was no luxury to them equal to this. There was not even a competing one.

Another analogous source of capital in early times was making slaves and breeding slaves. Yet neither in the capture nor in the breeding was there any kind of relinquishment of enjoyment. The slaves were gained in the fortune of war, and if A had not enslaved B, B would have enslaved A. The joy of the combat was, perhaps, the greatest known in those times. And even in the cruellest times it was probably pleasanter to spare the life of the captive than to take it.

A similar source is marriage, which, indeed, is all but the same, for even the highest wives of primitive ages worked in the house, much like slaves, and the concubines, who really were slaves, were but faintly divided from these wives. But it would be absurd to call keeping a harem a kind of abstinence, though harems were a great form of capital, and the members of them made a great deal of wealth.

The reason why we now so closely connect " abstinence" with capital is, that the final product of our industry is almost always received in what I may call an " optional" medium. Almost all our wealth is created to be exchanged, and that exchange is effected by means of money ; we can either use that money to buy perishable things which produce nothing, or we can " invest " it, as we say, in some producing business, or lend it to some one—generally to some one engaged in production—who will pay an interest upon it. But in a state of society where things are *not* created to be exchanged, " abstinence" plays no such constant part. Men must, it is true, abstain from eating the food which is necessary for their subsistence hereafter, and the food so obtained is, certainly, " capital " obtained by abstinence. But most permanent things which are made are like the " flint implement," and the primitive clay vessel, things which contribute to daily comfort because they are in daily use. The industry which created them never assumed an optional form, it was from the beginning fixed in the particular form in which it was created ; neither can be sold or exchanged, for we are supposing a state of society in which there is no exchange or sale.

A primitive patriarchal society is in fact very like this. Either exchange or sale was a very rare act in the lives of such persons as Lot or Abraham. They rarely saw any one to exchange with. They rarely went down into Egypt to buy anything; they rarely saw any sort of travelling merchant to whom they could sell anything. The life of such persons is a life of production, not for sale, but for use, as far as it is a life of production at all.

Hire is a still rarer phenomenon at such a period. Hire as a rule involves proximity of residence, so that the lender may be sure the hirer will return his article. If the borrower goes off to an unknown distance no one can be sure that he will do so. Nor for the most part is *trust*, which is essential in a loan, developed in societies till men have long lived near together, till they have learnt to know one another, and till they have created some sort of law, or formed some effectual custom which partly punishes and partly prevents bad faith. The diffused habit of lending things, which is the basis of so much of modern industry, is in truth a habit hard to diffuse, and one which the earliest men could not learn.

Nor even when the hire of capital does begin to be an important part of industrial organisation is there necessarily any abstinence from enjoyment in the possessor. Sir Henry Maine describes, in his *Early Institutions*, a condition of Irish society which was based on the loan of " cattle "—the main capital then existing—in which there was no abstinence in the lender at all. " Every considerable tribe," he tells us, " and almost every smaller body of men contained in it, is under a chief, whether he be one of the many tribal rulers whom the Irish records call kings, or whether he be one of those heads of joint families whom the Anglo-Irish lawyers at a later date called the Capita Cognationum. But he is not owner of the tribal land. His own land he may have, consisting of private estate or of official domain, or of both, and over the general tribal land he has a general administrative authority, which is ever growing greater over that portion of it which is unappropriated waste. He is meanwhile the military leader of his tribesmen, and, probably in that capacity, he has acquired great wealth in cattle. It has somehow become of great importance to him to place out portions of his herds among the tribesmen, and they on their part occasionally find themselves through stress of circumstance in pressing need of cattle for employment in tillage. Thus the chiefs appear in the Brehon law as perpetually ' giving stock,' and the tribesmen as receiving it. The remarkable thing is, that out of this practice grew, not only the familiar incidents of ownership, such as the right to rent and the liability to pay it, together with some other incidents less pleasantly familiar to the student of Irish history, but, above and besides these, nearly all the well-known incidents of feudal tenure. It is by taking stock that the free Irish tribesman becomes the Ceile or Kyle, the vassal or man of his chief, owing him not only rent but service and homage."

Upon the very surface of this description it is palpable that the chieftain gave up no enjoyment when he hired out these cattle ; he doubtless kept quite enough fully to feed himself with all his people, and after that he wanted no more. The power and place he gained by this *quasi* feudal use of them were the keenest kinds of pleasure then possible to him.

"Cattle" fill so subordinate a place in English industry that many English writers evidently never think of them when they speak of capital; they have in their minds the machines which they see; and they forget that once men bred capital more than they made it. Yet not only are cattle and capital, of course, etymologically the same word, but cattle fill a very curious place in the history of the subject.

First,—They are a kind of capital at once co-operative and remunerative; they can be used either to aid labour or to reward it; they are both helps to industry and means of pleasure. Their vital force is the best of early machines, and their milk and their flesh are the greatest of primitive luxuries. There is scarcely anything which primitive labourers more desire, and scarcely anything which helps them so much. And it is very curious that the sort of capital which first bore the name, and etymologically is the beginning of all the rest, should be a link between, and combine, the nature of two things, now so dissimilar, that at first it hardly seems right that they should have the same name,—the bread which the labourer eats and for which he works, and the spindle or the loom with which he works.

Secondly,—Cattle unquestionably, on account of this double desirability, are among the earliest forms of money, probably the very earliest in which "large transactions," as we should now speak, were settled. It was the first, or among the first, of "wholesale" moneys.

In this way, though English Political Economy often neglects the use of cattle as capital, and though some of its doctrines are inapplicable to "cattle" in the primitive condition of industry, cattle have nevertheless been a main agent in creating the developed state of industry in which English Political Economy was thought out, and to which alone it is entirely applicable. Cattle rendered possible primitive agriculture, which first kept men close together, and so made the division of labour possible; were the beginning of "wages-paying capital" which that "division" first requires and then extends; were among the first things hired, and the first money. We should be careful to watch in this single article the transitions of industry, for the so doing may save us from the greatest of all mistakes, that of riveting as a universal form upon all societies axioms only fitting societies like our own.

These illustrations might be multiplied almost endlessly, but what have been given are enough to prove that capital is created by any series of acts by which men make, or bring into existence, useful things, and that only some of these acts are accompanied by abstinence, while others are not.

Thirdly,—Neither is the loan of capital always accompanied by abstinence; it may or may not be according to circumstances.

. . . .

If, to simplify the matter, we look at the state of things which is going on around us, we see that capital augments in this way. People's incomes are paid in money; out of that money some is spent on necessary subsistence, some on temporary enjoyment, and some on durable means of comfort ; the rest is left in " money," and this we call the saving, the new " capital ". The amount of it depends on three elements, first, and evidently, on the amount of the income out of which the saving is to be made ; secondly, on the degree in which future wants preponderate over present ones ; and lastly, on the *efficiency* of saving, the *success* it obtains.

The first and greatest future want is what I may call the " old stocking " one, that is, the craving to have some stock of money laid against the unknown future. The strength of this craving differs much in various races of men ; and, as a rule, the strong races, used to prosperity, have much less of it than the weak ones familiar with adversity. You will find much more laid up in the cabin of an Irish peasant than in the cottage of an English artisan, though the latter has five times the greater means. And this is natural, because the English artisan believes, and probably believes with truth, that he is sure to be able to earn money ; whereas the Irishman's notions are based on a world where it has often been impossible to earn a farthing, and in which those ready to live even on potatoes could not get potatoes to live on. Even in higher life very considerable sums, for their circumstances, are often saved by timid, weak people. I know a case in which a sum of (I think) £120 was made up for a gentleman who had become incapacitated ; he enjoyed it a few years, and when he died from £700 to £800 were found in his room. He always feared that his income, or part of it, might cease, and wanted to be able to live if it did. Against all contingent evils this "stocking" fund is a resource, and against old age, the most likely of those evils. The next greatest—or probably an equally great—future want is the desire to provide for the next generation. People insure their lives who save in no other way. There is probably no greater anxiety in the world than the wish of parents to start children in the same level of life in which they started themselves, and few greater ambitions than to start them on a higher level. Lastly, there is the desire to be rich, especially in countries where wealth makes the man, where it not only buys commodities, but where without it some of the best unbought things—respect and deference—are not easy to be had. I need not enumerate the present wants which come into collision with these, nor go into any detail as to them.

But we must observe what is incessantly forgotten, that it is not a Spartan and ascetic state of society which most generates saving. On the contrary, if a whole society has few wants there is little motive for saving. The reserve, the old stocking store of those who want little, need only be small. Those who want to start their children with little, need save little ; those who reckon £100 a year "riches," need not, and will not, deprive themselves of anything to obtain more; a state of society which encourages that feeling is not likely to be rich. Nothing is commoner than to read homilies on luxury, because it is a "waste of money," and "bad for the poor".

But without the multifarious accumulation of wants which are called luxury, there would in such a state of society be far less saving than there is. If you look at the West-end of London with its myriad comforts and splendours, it looks at first sight like a mere apparatus for present enjoyment. And so far as the present feelings of those who live there go, it often is. Very many of the inhabitants are thinking only of themselves. But there is no greater benefit to the community for all that than this seemingly thoughtless enjoyment. It is the bait by which the fish is caught; it is the attraction by which capital is caught. To lead a bright life like that, at least that their children may lead it or something like it, many times as many as those who now live it, spare and save. And if it be good for the poor that capital should be saved, then the momentary luxury which causes that saving, is good for the poor. The analogy of animal life is reversed, for it is the butter-fly which begins as the grub.

On the other side we must remember what, in books of Political Economy, is sometimes forgotten, that saving is not necessarily good. The capital may come too dear. A clergyman who gives his children a good education, does more really to increase wealth, not to say anything of anything else, than if he saved the money. The engineer, the lawyer, the physician, are in their various ways productive people; and the nation would have been poorer, not richer, if their father had kept the money which educated them, in order to leave them at his death so much more. The same may not be so conspicuously true of the daughters, but it is as much so really. A good mother of a family causes more wealth than half the men, for she trains from the beginning boys to be fit for the world, and to make wealth ; and if she fails at that beginning the boys will be worse gold finders all their lives.

It must be observed, too, that there is an intellectual element in the matter. Besides the two kinds of wants, future and present, there is the faculty of making the comparison. And the habits of some people's lives fit them much more for this than those of others. An actor who is concerned with the momentary impression on passing audiences has nothing to bring the future close to him at all. An artisan has little more ; his daily work passes with the day. But a capitalist in business has the future for ever brought home to him. He has to look into the future, perhaps a distant one, for the profit on the goods which he buys, and to find in the near future the money with which these goods are to be paid for. The first thing in his mind is a list of " acceptances " soon to be provided for ; the next is the balance-sheet to be made up sometime hence. A banker, above all men, incessantly lives in the future. He is, or ought to be, for ever thinking how he should pay his deposits if he were asked for them ; he must think daily how he will find means for the current demands of every day. He too has a balance-sheet to be looked to upon the results of which he will have to live. A man thus living in the future, has a greater disposition to provide for it. And this is the one main reason why the man of business, of whatever species—the manufacturer, the merchant, or the banker—will save much more than any kind of person who lives upon the fruits of a momentary skill or talent.

In many minds this feeling coalesces with the "old stocking want"—that is to say, the desire to provide for definite engagements, those engagements being an incessant series, passes into and is blended with the desire to provide for the unknown. The pecuniary classes have a general feeling of "liability" about their minds to which other classes are strangers. And justly, because their risks, not only their known, but their unknown ones, are greater. I once heard a very experienced man lay down this principle: "A man of business," he said, "ought not to be over cautious; he ought to take what seem good things in his trade pretty much as they come; he won't get any good by trying to see through a millstone. But he ought to put all his caution into his 'reserve fund'; he may depend on it he will be 'done' somehow before long, and probably when he least thinks it; he ought to heap up a great fund in a shape in which he can use it, against the day at which he wants it." It is the disposition so generated, which is in a trading nation among the strongest motives to save.

Besides these two factors in the growth of capital, the amount of the income out of which saving has to be made, and the disposition to sacrifice what is present to what is future, there is, I have said, a third, *viz.*, the efficiency of saving in creating capital. There is a whole scale of various degrees of this efficiency in actual life. At the bottom is the brisk peasant who puts away his money into an old stocking, who has no means of employing it, who will not trust any one else with it. Here, all that the saving of £10 will produce is £10; it is sure never to get any more. At the top of the scale is the able capitalist in a large and growing business; every penny he can put into it yields him a high profit, because he gets an income from unusual ability, unusual opportunity, as well as the common rate. Such a man will almost always save more than others, because he has a far greater reward *per cent.* for saving it. The rate of profit depends on the efficiency of industry. When more is made at less cost, the profit is greater; when less at greater, the profit is less. I am not sure whether, to many minds, this language will not present a difficulty. I know it long did so to my own. I was conscious of a haze about it. " It is stated," I said to myself, "that there is ' more' of something or other, but of *what* is there more ? " And I could not answer the question very well. More " exchangeable value," more " money's worth," were the natural answers, but I was not satisfied that they were the complete ones. We must analyse a little further. The easiest case to analyse is the gold-mining, the money-making business. If 10,000 sovereigns are invested in gold-mining—in paying wages, in buying machinery, and in accompanying expenses—and if that produce per annum, gold, which can be made into £11,000, this measures the rate of profit in the country. If the efficiency of industry were less, so many additional sovereigns would not be produced; if more, a proportionately greater number would be produced. In the profit of all trades there is the same fundamental fact; an addition to the "exchangeable value" of the commodities of a country; but in the profit of the gold-mining business we can see that fact most easily, because we can take the capital before it is invested as so much gold, and it comes back as that much, *plus* some more. In other cases there is a change necessary into money, in this case the profit palpably results from the mere production.

We must observe, however, that this profit in the gold-mining trade is only a measure of the general rate of profit in the country, and of the general efficiency of industry which causes that rate; it has no peculiarity about it, except that which has been said. If the profit in this trade were more than in any other, capital would go thither, the production of gold would augment, and prices, measured in gold, would rise. This would raise the price of gold-mining machinery, the rate of gold-miners' wages, and all the incidental out-goings of the trade. And, as the number of sovereigns which that "machinery" and those "miners" could produce is not increased, the profit in the trade will fall. And the reverse will happen if that profit be less. A contrary series of changes will make it rise.

In a country in which the productive arts are high, other things being equal, profits will be high also. If the outlay of the capitalist on all means of production is the same, his remuneration will be greatest where more is produced. Suppose by a sudden series of inventions the productive power of industry were augmented in all trades ten per cent. (including the gold-mining trade, so that we may be clear of all questions as to money and price), the revenue of the capitalist would be augmented by that ten per cent., on condition of course of his outlay in all ways remaining the same, including that on wages ; and his power of saving would be augmented equally.

Single sudden inventions which help in everything, do not happen, but the general progress of the productive arts in the last thirty years has been very like it, as far as effects go. Almost everything has been made more easily ; many things far more easily. Even the growth of raw produce for sale has been facilitated, if not as much as some other things, yet still very much. Railways have made land which was far from the market able to compete with that near it. The daily subsistence of such a city as London would have been excessively costly in the pre-railway time, perhaps it would have been impossible. The amount of things produced on purpose to be exchanged now, as compared with fifty years ago, is so much increased that our fathers would not have comprehended it or believed it. The rise of prices would have been enormous, if the same extension of productive power had not extended to the money trades, to gold and silver. For many years before 1840 the production of these metals had been excessively slow, and their value was rising. Mr. Jevons thinks " that prices had on the average fallen between the years 1820 and 1844 in the ratio of 103

to 69, or by 33 per cent., whereas between 1844 and
1857 they rose in the ratio of 69 to 85, or by about
23 per cent.".[1]   Thus the effect of the great gold
discoveries consisted more in arresting the previous
continuous *appreciation* of the precious metals than in
causing a positive depreciation.   Indeed, in 1863,
Mr. Jevons stated the depreciation of gold at the
very moderate amount of 13 to 16 per cent.[2]

If the increase in the productive power of general
industry had come upon an age straitened as to
money-making industry, the fall of prices would have
been such as we have no example of, and the effects
would have been harassing and confusing.   But
fortunately the production of gold and silver has been
even more facilitated than that of most other things.
There has been no such confusing fall of prices, as,
except for the new discoveries of gold in California
and Australia, there would have been.   The effect of
the productiveness of industry has been greatly to
retard and almost to prevent the equally confusing
rise of prices, which would otherwise have happened.
The productive power of men of business has thus
been incalculably augmented, and with that their
saving power.

The second main source of capital in the present
day is the saving of men—of persons out of business.
Such persons not being able to make anything themselves must put such part of their income as they
wish to save into the hands of others, and far the
most important way in which they do this is by

---

[1] *Journal of the London Statistical Society*, vol. xxviii., p. 315.
[2] *Serious Fall in the Value of Gold*, etc., p. 30.

lending. They lend it on interest, and what they can save varies, other things being the same, with that interest. What then will that amount be ? This is determined as other market prices are determined.[1]

The most important factors in fixing it are the amounts of money to be lent, and the amounts which borrowers are willing to borrow upon such security as the lenders are willing to accept. The most important of these borrowers are men of business. These will be most anxious to borrow money when the rate of profit is high, and when, therefore, they can employ it to the most advantage ; at such times they will strain every nerve to obtain as much as possible. But in the earlier states of industry they have great difficulty in obtaining it. They have no security which will satisfy those who wish to lend. In such epochs, the only sort of " security," the only way in which the borrower can make the lender sure of his money, is by depositing with him fixed property, or at least giving him the control over it. He must pledge movables, or transfer the *indicia* of ownership over immovables. But in such a commercial civilisation as ours, there is an immense and very powerful machinery for conducting the money of the accumulating class into the hands of the using class. Bankers and bill-brokers form a class whose business it is to know the credit of different persons, and to say when and how far they singly, or together, can be trusted. Millions are lent in this country upon bills of exchange with only two signatures—that is

[1]See Note A on Market Price at the end of the volume.

upon an order to pay money accepted by the person
to whom it is addressed, and which the person who
gives the order engages to pay if the other does not.
The money is, therefore, in fact, advanced on an
estimated probability that one or other of these two
persons will pay, of which the skilled advancing class
—the bankers and the bill-brokers—form their judgment. We are so familiar with it that we forget
how marvellous it is. But probably our modern
civilisation, notwithstanding its railways, telegraphs,
and other like things, has nothing similar. That an
endless succession of slips of written promises should
be turned into money as readily as if they were
precious stones, would have seemed incredible in
commerce till very recent times. Our ancestors
would have understood that something like it might
happen with the promises of a few millionaires or
Governments, but they would have never thought it
possible that such an infinity of names could be
known, or promises estimated. And the wonder is
greater because they are not estimated equally; the,
relative possibility of different " parties " not paying
is materially determined to the minutest gradations;
and a bill is done at $3\frac{7}{8}$ or 4 per cent. accordingly.
The intermediate dealers — the bill-brokers and
bankers—live upon this knowledge; they gain if they
are right, and are ruined if they are often much
wrong; and, therefore, they *are* right. Through
these expedients an immense tide of money flows into
commerce at most times, though occasionally they
are impaired, and it is impeded.

Our commercial civilisation also tends more and

more to improve the means by which actual property can be pledged. The *indicia* of ownership are made more easily transferable. The English law of real property does not bear a very good reputation, but it is indisputable that in this respect it is more advanced than any similar law in the world. In the last century the Courts of Equity decided that the deposit of title-deeds with, or even without, a written memorandum was an adequate security for a loan. And on this sort of "equitable" mortgage a very large sum is lent for short periods, especially by country bankers, who know the people to whom, and the land on which, they are lending. Most individual transactions of this sort are small, but the sum total is very great. Dock and warehouse warrants for goods deposited are also fruits and indications of a highly improved commercial state. They, and all similar means of pledging property, tend to augment the borrowing power of men of business, and so to raise the rate of interest.

Besides men of business, who borrow in order to *make,* a large class of people borrow in order to *hold.* The pride and pleasure of possessing property are so great that people will very often pledge that property in order to obtain it. A large part of the titles of our richest landowners are mortgaged in this way to "insurance offices," who have much money constantly to lend. The arrangement suits both parties, for no one knows of the loan; as the insurance office is permanent, the loan is rarely called in, and thus the landowner gets the pomp of ownership, while the office enjoys the perfection of a security.

There is also a class of persons who borrow in order to spend, that is, to spend the principal (for all borrowers spend the interest, else they would not want to borrow). In such countries as England, where the producing and the preserving classes are such large borrowers, the demand of spendthrifts has but little influence on the rate of interest. It is overpowered by the comparative greatness of other demands. But in simpler states of society the demand of the "prodigal" fills a conspicuous place in the money market, and in some of the books which have come down to us from those early times he seems the principal borrower that is thought of. But the growth of civilisation, though diminishing this species of spending borrowers, creates another much more efficient species. Governments obtain a vast credit, and borrow for war and other non-productive purposes, such as in the early history of mankind could never have been imagined. The loss of France by individual "prodigals" will not, for ages, be as great as her loss by the folly of the seven months' war with Germany. This is, of course, so much to be deducted from the capital of the country, but nevertheless the sum so borrowed tends to raise the rate of interest, and thus to augment the means of future saving by those who wish to save.

At the present day, therefore, the amount of saving in a nation depends, as we have seen, on the amount of the annual income out of which saving is to be made. The disposition to save out of it (varying in different classes), and the efficiency of

saving, in creating new capital, depend partly on
the rate of profit and partly on the rate of interest.
And from this saving arises the annual increment of
capital—the amount of yearly addition to it; but
there is also a yearly decrement—an annual waste.
The amount of this depends in such a country as
England mainly on the amount of unsuccessfulness,
of absolute loss in business. Certain adventures not
only bring no profit, but never return the capital
spent on them. The liabilities of bankruptcy estates
in England, including liquidations and composi-
tions, but excluding public companies, in 1870 were
£17,456,000 ; the apparent assets were £5,382,000 ;
the difference therefore, or £12,074,000, was so
much pure loss. And there is much other loss in
business which does not figure here.

To this must be added the loss in such a country
and age as ours—usually loss by private prodigals
and by State follies. If we could only know the
amount of the diminutions and augmentations in
any nation, could deduct the one from the other, we
should know the increase of the capital during this
time by that nation.

We must be careful, however, to observe that our
account of the growth of capital is only applicable to
such times as ours—to times when the division of
labour has been carried out, and where almost everything is produced by one man for sale to others.
The result of this is that every sale changes a man's
product into a form in which he has the choice of
saving or not saving it. The money which is the
proceed of the sale may either be spent on immediate

enjoyment, or set aside in some way for the future. The incomes of men are in an adult economic society received in an *optional* medium. But in early societies this is not so. Things not being produced for sale are only what they are by nature; there is no choice in the way of using most of them; they are by their essential character either fit for present use, or fit to be set apart for the future. They are very rarely in the same degree fit for both. Defoe illustrates this better than many graver authors.

Our account of the growth of capital also assumes that men can always find something to save in, that a person who wants to provide for his future wants, can do so if he will give up present ones. But this is not true in early times at all. Most primitive wants are for rapidly perishable things; and it is of no use to keep a store of those things. If you do, you will be "keeping stale fish," you will have sacrificed the present without obtaining the future; you will have that which was of use once, but now is so no longer. "Food" is the greatest want of early times. But most food—vegetable or animal— will not of itself last long. It is of no use for a tribe of hunters to set aside the game they kill. It is not till the pastoral age has arrived that men have any means of storing up the food they require. The first "granaries" of men were, if the phrase be allowed, "live granaries"; the flocks and herds which walked the fields, and could be left, when not wanted to be slaughtered, where they were. Clothes, the second great want of man, are always short-lived, and it is not much use to store them up. There was, in early times, no mode of supplying those wants for the future; men had to live from hand to mouth.

COST OF PRODUCTION.

I.

MANY persons are much puzzled by the phrase exchangeable value—not only outsiders and learners, but even practical thinkers on the subject use it awkwardly, and do not feel that the idea is vivid in their minds. And, if we look at the matter historically, it is very natural that this should be so. No nation—no set of persons—who did not possess a fixed and efficient money ever attained the idea. Nations which only use barter know that a certain amount of one or two common things mostly exchanges for a certain amount of one or two other things;—but they have no conception of the "value" of one thing as against *all* other things. This idea is only gained by the use of money as a general common measure. By measuring all things —not one—against one, men come to be able to measure them against one another. "Price"—price in money—is the foundation of the economic idea of exchangeable value. But though it is the foundation of that idea, it is not the whole of it. "Money" is a commodity like any other, and it tends to fluctuate in the ratios in which it exchanges with other commodities, from chances affecting itself, just as they do in relation to it. At any single moment if you know the "prices" of all articles, you know their relative exchangeable value. But when you come to compare one time with another—say, the prices of to-day with those of this time last year— you might be much puzzled, for possibly all might have risen, or all might have fallen. And this would have arisen not from anything which related to the things measured, but from something affect- ing the measuring instruments. What we mean by exchangeable value in Political Economy is not actual price, but perfect price,—the ratio in which everything exchanges against all other things— measured, not, as it is, by the intrinsically valuable measure of money, but as it would be against a similar measure which was invariable intrinsically.

We must bear in mind that on no two days, indeed at no two minutes, are the rates at which things exchange for one another at all the same. The price list of the Stock Exchange varies from hour to hour, and so do the prices in other markets. General "exchangeable value," which is the sum total of price lists, is, therefore, incessantly altering. The fact which it denotes is one of the greatest complexity with which any science can have to deal, and it is no wonder, therefore, that most imagina- tions find it hard to get and keep a hold of it. Incomparably the best way to aid them in this, is to make an hypothesis, and to assume that money is of invariable value. Of course this is an hypo- thesis not coinciding with fact. On the contrary, it leaves out a whole range of facts. But if we are careful with it—if we remember what are the omitted facts, and make corrections for them if necessary—

the hypothesis is of the greatest use. The figures
of price are, in this case, like the symbols of Algebra ;
they hedge-in the mind to a definite thought.

But as a matter of fact, in markets, though monetary changes of price are incessant, yet general relations are constant ; and in a former page we saw
that in relation to articles which human industry can
indefinitely multiply, and which it does so multiply
for the hope of profit, and within a " nation " in
the economic sense—that is, a group of producers
within which labour and capital freely circulate—
these constant relations are fixed by the " cost of
production ". What, then, is this cost accurately ?
It is in relation to this that we shall find the hypothesis as to fixed value of money especially useful
All other modes of dealing with the subject are apt
to leave the mind of the reader somewhat dull and
stupid, and to make him, though convinced at each
step of the reasonings, not quite sure of the effect of
the whole.

This cost of production in a mature state of
industry and where there is a strict division of
persons into capitalists, artisans, and labourers, is
the cost at which it would " pay " a capitalist to
produce a given product, and the word " pay " means
that he must have his " outlay," the money he has
expended, returned to him, and that he must have,
over and above, so much, by way of profit—so
much " to the good," as we commonly speak—as
will induce him to make the production. Translated
into more abstract language, you can say that the
capitalist must be in possession, or have the means

of possessing himself, of certain articles, possessing exchangeable value; that those articles are parted with, or destroyed in making the product, and that he must have articles of equal exchangeable value returned to him by the exchange of his product, together with a profit. But though a most valuable way of speaking for some purposes, for those of common exposition, this abstract way is inferior to the more concrete way.

A great deal of the indistinctness which often hovers round the subject arises because those who think of it do not enough trace the matter as it runs through the mind of the capitalist. In our modern production all depends on him. It is he who settles what undertakings shall be embarked in, and what not; which things shall be made and which left unmade. The price at which a thing can be bought is the price at which the capitalist will undertake to lay it down; if you want to know why one thing is cheap and another dear, you must analyse in each case the calculations of the capitalist.

The first and most obvious thing which a capitalist must do, is to pay his wages. Labour—the muscular and mental force of man—is a main element in almost all kinds of production, and the principal one in many. But we must be careful not to imagine that this labour which the capitalist purchases is one thing. It is hardly even one *kind* of thing. The labour of a ploughman is distinct from that of a clerk; that of a clerk from that of an engine-driver; that of an engine-driver from that of a cabinet-maker, and so on without end. The difference

between these various kinds of labour is in a great
degree the consequence of acquired habit.　Each
man is trained in his department, and in it, therefore, he acquires a skill.　These various kinds of
training go down to very low degrees—to the "navvy,"
who just knows how to dig out plain earth,—and
runs up to the most accomplished artisan—the
maker of astronomical instruments (say) who can
turn out work of the finest and most minute
accuracy, and to a great extent knows how he does
it, and how that accuracy is acquired.　There is a
common coarse sort of human nature which can be
taken a certain way in any pursuit, but which will
not go very far ; and over and above that, there is
a finer element which can only be taken in one
direction, or some few directions for which it has
an affinity, and which is often accompanied by an
incompetence to go even the first step in many
others.　Out of these natures specifically inclined
to it, each trade gets its best labourers.　The capitalist in each line has to try the various sorts, if he
can get them, and to pay higher for the finer sorts.
I say, *if* he can get them, because a main key to the
reason why industries are distributed apparently so
capriciously over the face of the country, is to be
found in the power of being able to buy easily and
cheaply *all* the kinds of labour which each kind of
trade wants.　In a place where a trade has long
been carried on, all these tend to accumulate ; a
family tradition carries them on from father to son,
and the whole mind of the place comes to be full of
it.　The language of the district soon assumes that

you know it, and those who do not are a kind of aliens. "As water" in all cases "comes to the river," so the place where a trade has long been carried on tends to attract those who by nature like that trade, and feel that they are fitted for it. Thus commerce, ,which, being wholly of human creation, one might have fancied to be very mutable, is really a thing most conservative. It will stay in a place for very many years which has given no natural facility to it,—often which seems to have interposed a difficulty. To get all the kinds of skill suitable for a trade in their proper proportions is a long task, requiring many years; a new place cannot have it for a long time, and an old place for a long time will be superior in this cardinal advantage.

One special kind of labour which almost every capitalist must have more or less of, is what we call his "establishment"; that is, his head men who transmit his orders, or give them to his corresponding clerks; his book-keeping clerks, who keep what we may call his "memory"; and the result of their labour shows what has become of his capital, and whether he is getting or losing. In some trades, as in banking, and some other distributive trades, this kind of charge is one of the greatest; and almost all people in a very large way of business have a large staff of confidential persons whom they know and who know them, and who work together with an efficiency, though often incessantly "having words," which no casual gang suddenly collected can for an instant compete with.

Next, a capitalist must buy his "machines". And there is no reason to take up time and space with saying how various and wonderful they are at the present day. Everybody will remember that, without its being said. What is much more to our present purpose is to say that outlay on wages has a different effect on the price of commodities from an outlay on machinery. If £100,000 is laid out during the year in wages, that sum must all be returned by the sale of the articles produced in the year. But that is not true of an outlay on machinery. On the contrary, £100,000 laid out in machinery need not all come back so soon. The machinery will last for years,— and the capitalist does not want to have the first outlay returned to him till the very end, when it is quite worn out. Money spent on wages is a lump sum, which the products of the year must return; money spent on machinery a sum repayable by terminable annuity, extending over all the years the machine lasts. Each cotton shirting must by its sale recoup the capitalist for the wages spent in making it; but it need only return to him a small fraction of the cost of the machinery by which it was made, because that machinery will go on making shirtings for many years, and it is the aggregate which must make the return to the capitalist, and not any one.

Machine-making, it is to be observed, is a trade which especially tends to adhere to particular places, because more than any other trade it requires the easy and cheap supply of the exact kind of skilled labour in the exact quantity in which it is wanted.

And this you cannot have in a new place. A machine-making factory which would thrive at Birmingham, would starve at the Land's End.

Next, a capitalist must mend his machinery; and this is the most conservative force of all. The number of subsidiary trades which any one great manufacture requires merely to keep its plant going, is very large, and in out-of-the-way spots no one of them, of course, exists. They only grow round the principal trade gradually, and as time goes on. And many of them are subsidiary to several trades. The place, therefore, which has longest had possession of such trades has an incalculable advantage, as far as this item is concerned.

Next, the capitalist, having bought his machinery, must buy the power of moving that machinery. And this is a point on which very many people have no clear notions; there is a difficulty in comprehending the difference between the two,—a disposition to confound force and wheels. In the old times of watermills and windmills, I am inclined to think that the distinction was clearer; it was then patent that the most elaborate machinery would not move unless there was some external force to push it. But the use of coal has rather mystified the matter. People do not see the pushing power, and therefore they do not believe that it exists. A steam-engine is so large and complex a thing that people in general have no real idea how it moves. The truth of course is that the burning of the coal heats the water, that the heating of the water causes it to expand, that this expansion gives a "shove," and that all the rest of the machine only transmits and passes on that "shove". You must have something like this to start with—something that will produce a pressure, or you cannot move your machinery at all. I have known highly experienced men of business, however, who are very far from clear about this. In discussion as to the consequences of the extinction of our "coal," nothing is more common than to hear it said : "Oh, then we must adopt new forms of machinery". You might as well try by improving and educating the mothers to continue a species without fathers. There is a certain motive "power" in nature which is as essential as any matter to be moved.

This element in the cost of production tends quite in the opposite way to the previous ones; it tends not to keep trade where it is, but to make it move. The best coal mines, the best sources of power of all kinds in each district, are soon appropriated and used. The natural tendency of trade, as far as this element in the cost of production guides it, would be to move incessantly over the face of the world, always touching the best sources of power only—the quickest water-courses, the most exposed sites for windmills, the best coal mines,—and never stopping to exhaust the second-rate sources.

Next, the capitalist must buy the materials which he is to work up with this power and this machinery. And the effect of this item, too, is just like the last. It tends to migration. The principal materials of industry are the tissues of vegetables, the fleeces and skins of animals, and the products of mines. And commerce is for ever hunting out the places at which such animals can be reared, such vegetables grown, and such minerals extracted. New places are constantly being discovered where these can be done, and manufactures, if not tied by the other items of cost, would be for ever stimulated to move by this one. Then the capitalist must rent the land on which his factory is built, or on which his business is carried on, and what the laws are by which this is regulated we have seen.

Next, he must pay interest on as much of his capital as he finds it convenient to borrow, and as he can get the loan of. And this is a steady cause operating in favour of old countries, because capital has there accumulated and is cheap, whereas in new countries it is still scarce and cannot be borrowed, except at great cost, if at all. As commerce becomes involved and credit complex, more and more of business tends to be carried on with borrowed money; and the comparative cheapness of it in established places of industry is one of the reasons why trades stay there as they do,—why so many of them are stationary, and so few migratory.

Lastly, in many cases, though not in all, the capitalist must make known the goodness—or, at least, must allege the goodness—of his work. Advertising is a kind of outlay which to some extent is essential in all trades, and it takes different forms. A company which hires a showy shop front, a broker who is for ever sending round trade circulars, are really advertising just as much as dealers who insert in the newspapers puffs of their articles; the end in all cases is to sell something, and in the long run the buyer pays for it all.

I have been speaking as if all products were made or manufactured. Common language has no apt expressions for the general ideas of Political Economy. There is no easy mode of describing all the processes by which all sorts of articles are changed by men from the state in which they are worth less, into that in which they are worth more. The case of a manufacturer is the simplest case to the imagination, and I have, therefore, taken it as the standard. Besides it, there are the breeding of animals, the growth of vegetables, and the extraction of minerals; but any one who has analysed the outlay of the capitalist in manufactures will have no difficulty in doing so for the others ;—*mutatis mutandis* it all comes to the same thing, though the words of describing it differ. In all, the capitalist will have to pay wages ; to buy co-operative instruments (animals included) ; to obtain a site ; probably to borrow capital ; probably to make known the value of his article. His outlay will be on these ; and what he has over, after replacing these, is profit. The whole of business in great commercial countries is that of a replacement, with an addition of capital. As a rule, the capitalists of a trade must have their capital returned to them with the profit of the country, or they will not continue in that trade.

II.

One result of these truths is, I think, to clear up the most abstruse discussion in which English Political

Economy has recently been engaged—the discussion which Mr. Cairnes raised against Mr. Mill on the "cost of production". And this result is just of the kind which might be expected, for it is in the beginning of arguments that their difficulties are hidden and any one who will really go back to that beginning will be sure to meet his reward. Let us look at the matter a little carefully.

When any article, say a steam-engine, is in our modern state of industry produced by a capitalist maker, it is necessary to repay to that capitalist maker all which he has expended upon it ; if it cost £500, and the current rate of profit be a 10 per cent. rate, he must have £550. His capital must be returned to him, and he must have the remuneration for that capital for the risk of losing it, for the trouble of managing it, and so on. But Mr. Mill takes his analysis further. He analyses the cost of production into the "wages of labour," and the "profits of capital," and after speaking of the former, thus proceeds : " Thus far of labour, or wages, as an element in cost of production. But in our analysis, in the First Book, of the requisites of production we found that there is another necessary element in it besides labour. There is also capital ; and this being the result of abstinence, the produce, or its value, must be sufficient to remunerate, not only all the labour required, but the abstinence of all the persons by whom the remuneration of the different classes of labourers was advanced. The return for abstinence is profit. And profit, we have also seen, is not exclusively the surplus remaining to the capitalist after he has been compensated for his outlay, but forms, in most cases, no unimportant part of the outlay itself. The flax-spinner, part of whose expenses consists of the purchase of flax and of machinery, has had to pay, in their price, not only the wages of the labour by which the flax was grown and the machinery made, but the profits of the grower, the flax-dresser, the miner, the iron-founder, and the machine-maker. All these profits, together with those of the spinner himself, were again advanced by the weaver, in the price of his material —linen yarn ; and along with them the profits of a fresh set of machine-makers, and of the miners and ironworkers who supplied them with their metallic material. All these advances form part of the cost of production of linen. Profits, therefore, as well as wages, enter into the cost of production which determines the value of the produce."

But this reasoning assumes that all capital comes from " abstinence," whereas a great deal of it does not. What the capitalist in this case really hires is the use of the past plant of the world, whatever its origin. Thus the steam-engine maker hires the use of a whole series of tools and things, going back to the first flint implements, and the first tamed animals. In the first beginnings of that series—the link on which it all hangs—there was no relinquishment of any enjoyment. There was no such " abstaining," as Mr. Mill supposes, and therefore Mr. Mill's analysis fails. He takes us back into a hypothetical history which he does not prove, and which he could not prove, for it is not true.

Further, Mr. Mill's analysis supposes the present organisation of industry—that in which the capitalist buys the force of the labourer and pays him wages—to be the one which began at the beginning. Mr. Mill says: "What the production of a thing costs to its producer, or its series of producers, is the labour expended in producing it. If we consider as the producer the capitalist who makes the advances, the word 'labour' may be replaced by the word 'wages': what the produce costs to him, is the wages which he has had to pay. At the first glance, indeed, this seems to be only a part of his outlay, since he has not only paid wages to labourers, but has likewise provided them with tools, materials, and perhaps buildings. These tools, materials, and buildings, however, were produced by labour and capital; and their value, like that of the article to the production of which they are subservient, depends on cost of production, which again is resolvable into labour. The cost of production of broadcloth does not wholly consist in the wages of weavers; which alone are directly paid by the cloth manufacturer. It consists also of the wages of spinners and wool-combers, and, it may be added, of shepherds, all of which the clothier has paid for in the price of yarn. It consists, too, of the wages of builders and brick-makers, which he has reimbursed in the contract price of erecting his factory. It partly consists of the wages of machine-makers, iron-founders, and miners. And to these must be added the wages of the carriers who transported any of the means and appliances of the production to the place where they were to be used, and the product itself to the place where it is to be sold."

This principle, as applied to existing societies, may seem very obvious; indeed, it is most commonly assumed in popular discussions, both as being true and as being the principle of English Political Economy. But, nevertheless, most eminent Political Economists refuse to regard it as ultimate, and try to get behind it. And, no doubt, in one sense it is not ultimate. There are processes acting on value of which it does not take account. For example, the wages of similar labour tend—though slowly— to be equal in all employments, and it is contended that you ought not to say that the exchange value of an article has arrived at its "cost value" while the wages paid in its production are greater or less than those paid to similar labourers in other employments. Again, the wages of dissimilar kinds of labour bear, as a rule, some kind of proportion to one another (though the exceptions to this rule are in all societies many, and though some of them last for a very long time), and it is said that we have not arrived at the "cost value" of any article until, in the case of that article, the different species of labour are rewarded in the same proportion that they are in the case of other articles. And, no doubt, if we choose, we may thus define "cost value"; we may say that it is not realised till these conditions are satisfied. But if we do, we must go further, and regard "cost value" as an ideal limit, rather than as any actual thing at all. In truth the conception of the universal influence of the capitalist-employer is essentially modern. We have seen before that capital is scarce in new countries, that it moves slowly, and that the labourer and the capitalist are often one and the same. There is no such separate outlay as Mr. Mill's analysis presumes, and as our modern practice exhibits. On a large scale no such thing is possible till a good available money exists in which wages can be paid; and such a money did not begin till the human race had been working and labouring for many hundred years.

Mr. Mill's attempt to answer the question, " What is the cost of production which determines value ? " by saying that it is the sum of the wages of labour and profits and abstinence since the beginning of history, fails therefore at both its cardinal points— for in the beginning of history there was much capital yielding profit which did not come from abstinence, and much labour which was not paid by wages; and this capital and this labour were the seeds of all which now is, and must be reckoned in the list of things that made it, if we add up those things.

Nor do I think that Mr. Cairnes, most acute as he is here, as always, at all mends the matter. He says "that Mr. Mill was wrong in adding up past wages and past profits so as to make a total 'cost of production,' for that neither 'wages nor profits' are properly part of that cost at all". He tells us: " Of all ideas within the range of economic speculation, the two most profoundly opposed to each other are cost and the reward of cost,—the sacrifice incurred by man in productive industry, and the return made by nature to man upon that sacrifice. All industrial progress consists in altering the proportion between these two things; in increasing the remuneration in relation to the cost, or in diminishing the cost in relation to the remuneration. Cost and remuneration are thus economic antitheses of each other; so completely so, that a small cost and a large remuneration are exactly equivalent expressions. Now in the analysis of cost of production which I have quoted, these two opposites are identified; and cost, which is sacrifice, cost, which is what man pays to Nature for her industrial rewards, is said to consist of wages and profits, that is to say, of what Nature yields to man in return for his industrial sacrifices. The theory thus in its simple statement confounds opposite facts and ideas, and further examination will show that it involves conclusions no less perplexed, and in conflict with doctrines the most received."

But the "cost of production," in the sense in which that cost determines market value, means the "cost" to the person who brings it to that market. In England, at present, the capitalist pays the wages, and he will not do it unless he earns the profit. These pecuniary items are certainly elements in *price*, and "exchangeable value" is only an abstract word for a perfect price—a price which would never alter by changes in the money medium —and changes in which, accordingly, would show accurately the changes in the buying power of things. The pecuniary remuneration to the labourer, and the pecuniary remuneration of the capitalist, seem to me to be essential ingredients in the permanent money price which is to pay them both, for that price must permanently be such as will so pay them, and so pay them adequately.

Again, I do not think that abstinence and labour, or the rewards of them, are the sole elements in the existing cost of production. There is a third, which I call the hire of the present plant—of the existing productive things in the world. Suppose that a man goes into business with borrowed capital only, he will have to pay the "compensation" to abstinence, that is, the interest on capital to the man who lends him the money, and he will have likewise to hire labourers and pay them their wages. But besides this, he will have to hire machines to make his things. I say hire, not buy, for as far as the "cost of production" goes, this word gives more readily the required idea. A capitalist who has bought his machine gets back his money by an annuity; in the price of each bale of goods which he sells he includes a fraction of that annuity. It is as if he hired the machine and paid so much per bale as a rent or royalty for using it. When he buys the machine he commutes this royalty for a sum down. But he must get it repaid him annually for all that. And this repayment is so much to be added to the interest which he pays on his borrowed capital, and to what he pays in wages. It is an outlay which is a compensation neither for abstinence nor labour.

Cairnes would probably have said that as all the machines so hired were produced once by abstinence and labour, the hire of them was really a compensation to that past abstinence and labour. But here historical investigation again helps us. We have seen that the existing producing things of the world are the growth of a long history—that they are the product of many things, and that they cannot be set down as the products of simple abstinence and simple labour. If you resort to, an historical explanation, the first requirement is that the history must be true. No hypothesis or set of abstractions can help here. The appeal is to what has happened in matter of fact, and what is said to have thus happened never did so. And you cannot even confine such reasoning to somewhat developed states of society, for the very essence of this reasoning is to go back into the past and to assume that the cause of economic production has been uniform —has always been the product of the same two stated agencies.

And not only are the real facts of the growth of wealth thus inconsistent with the analysis which both Mill and Cairnes give us of the "cost of production," but they are still more inconsistent with the analysis of that cost which was generally held by the preceding generation of English Economists, and which is constantly to be found in the writings of Ricardo, though what seems to me to be a truer view is, as I shall presently show, to be found there also. This older analysis considers that "labour" is the sole source of value, and that all things of the same price have been produced by an equal quantity of "labour". But this older theory is evidently more unlike the facts than either of the newer ones. We have seen that these were not true, because they assumed that two factors—labour and abstinence—were the sole sources of wealth And *a fortiori* the older theory is untrue, for it assumes that a single factor—labour—has alone produced wealth.

III.

The difference which remains over in the hands of the capitalist is his profit. And this is a most essential element in the cost of production, for everything in developed trade depends on him. Unless he brings an article to market it will not be brought, and he will not bring it unless he has enough to repay him for what he does. And what he does is the most intellectual part of wealth—production and distribution. He is to the rest of the people so engaged what the general is to the army. It is he who settles what work operatives shall do, what sums clerks shall add up, how the managing men shall be employed. Not only does he save his capital and does not eat it, not only does he risk his capital, but he manipulates his capital. It is common to speak of the intellectual part of profit as the "wages of superintending wisdom". You might as well call whist superintending the cards. A man who plays cards very ill, will probably "play" his capital just as ill. The same kind of sagacity, the same observation, the same self-restraint are required in both. But though this is required of the capitalist, it is not all which is required. There is quite a different element besides. All business is in the nature of a game more or less difficult ; and requires the same sort of faculties, and the same kind of attention, as a game. But in most trades a capitalist has to govern others ; a large employer of labour has to govern many men. He has not only to move his pawns, but to rule his pawns. The pieces with which he plays are of flesh and blood, and will not move unless they like. He has to manage that they shall like. And, unless he is paid for all this, the article will not be made.

Ricardo was the first to give anything like this analysis of the cost of production. We have seen how imperfect, how confused, the analysis of Adam Smith was. Nor was there any great step in the matter made between his time and Ricardo's. The subject was not accurately worked out.

The analysis of Ricardo was, undoubtedly, defective, and he got himself into a difficulty of language which perplexes his writings and puzzles half his readers. Bentham said that he "confounded 'cost' and 'value'". And, in fact, having satisfied himself that things of equal cost of production will in the long run exchange for one another, he came to speak of the effect as if it were the cause, and of the cause as if it were the effect. I do not think he actually confused the two in thought, but he often seems to do so. Not being a highly educated man, he had, as has been said, a curious difficulty in the use of abstract lan-guage. He is like a mathematician in whose work there are a good many small inaccuracies, but whose work is still in the main right. Of course such a mathematician is a very imperfect one; the essence of mathematics is accuracy. In the same way Ricardo is a very imperfect abstract writer. The essence of abstract writing is precision, and in his use of abstract words he is defective in precision. Still the fault is of words only. When you come to examine the thought, you find that there was no obscurity in it; that it was perfectly clear in his mind.

It is a much worse fault that he only incompletely seized the notion that in an advanced state of society, where the capitalist brings the labour and offers the article for sale, the cost to the capitalist is that which regulates the value. No doubt, as we have seen, it is easy to imagine a simple society, where the labourers all support themselves — a set of hunters and weavers and fishers — where labour migrated from employment to employment just as one was better remunerated than another, and in which labour being the sole cost of production (that is to say, the labourers owning their own food and using their own tools), it was this migration which adjusted exchangeable value to cost. But there is a much quicker adjustment when capital is movable, and rapidly changes from employment to employment. What it costs the capitalist together with his profit settles the value. It does so, though the rate of wages for equal qualities of labour may be higher in one trade than another. As long as that is the case, the cost will be higher in the trade where wages are higher; and, therefore, the article produced will sell for more. In the end, labour will in most cases migrate from the badly paid to the well paid employment, and then the labour in both will be equally remunerated, and the price so far as it depends on labour will be the same. But even before this, the cost of production to the capitalist will regulate the price just as much as it does afterwards.

Ricardo might, more than any one else, have been expected to point this out, for he had an infinitely better perception of the quickness with which capital moves than any previous economist, and of the way in which it moves. "Whilst every man is free to employ his capital where he pleases, he will naturally seek for it that employment which is most advantageous; he will naturally be dissatisfied with a profit of 10 per cent., if by removing his capital he can obtain a profit of 15 per cent. This restless desire on the part of all the employers of stock, to quit a less profitable for a more advantageous business, has a strong tendency to equalise the rate of profits of all, or to fix them in such proportions as may, in the estimation of the parties, compensate for any advantage which one may have, or may appear to have, over the other. It is perhaps very difficult to trace the steps by which this change is effected; it is probably effected by a manufacturer not absolutely changing his employment, but only lessening the quantity of capital he has in that employment. In all rich countries, there is a number of men forming what is called the moneyed class; these men are engaged in no trade, but live on the interest of their money, which is employed in discounting bills, or in loans to the more industrious part of the community.

The bankers too employ a large capital on the same objects. The capital so employed forms a circulating capital of a large amount, and is employed, in larger or smaller proportions, by all the different trades of a country. There is perhaps no manufacturer, however rich, who limits his business to the extent that his own funds alone will allow; he has always some portion of this floating capital, increasing or diminishing according to the activity of the demand for his commodities. When the demand for silk increases, and that for cloth diminishes, the clothier does not remove with his capital to the silk trade, but he dismisses some of his workmen, he discontinues his demand for the loan from bankers and moneyed men; while the case of the silk manufacturer is the reverse: he wishes to employ more workmen, and thus his motive for borrowing is increased: he borrows more, and thus capital is transferred from one employment to another, without the necessity of a manufacturer discontinuing his usual occupation. When we look to the markets of a large town, and observe how regularly they are supplied both with home and foreign commodities, in the quantity in which they are required, under all the circumstances of varying demand, arising from the caprice of taste, or a change in the amount of population, without often producing either the effects of a glut from a too abundant supply, or an enormously high price from the supply being unequal to the demand, we must confess that the principle which apportions capital to each trade in the precise amount that it is required, is more active than is generally supposed."

From this passage it would have been expected that Ricardo would have said that in the state of industry with which he was here dealing, the cost of production which determines the price was the outlay of the capitalist, *plus* his profit, and that he would so have shown the subject in its true simplicity. But though in many passages he approaches to this clearness, though continually you seem to see the thought in his mind, he never quite utters it. You can nowhere find it in words. The difficulty of applying to real life the doctrine of cost of production, when otherwise explained, comes out in the following passage. "In speaking," says Ricardo, "however, of labour as being the foundation of all value, and the relative quantity of labour as almost exclusively determining the relative value of commodities, I must not be supposed to be inattentive to the different qualities of labour, and the difficulty of comparing an hour's or a day's labour, in one employment, with the same duration of labour in another. The estimation in which different qualities of labour are held, comes soon to be adjusted in the market with sufficient precision for all practical purposes, and depends much on the comparative skill of the labourer, and intensity of the labour performed. The scale, when once formed, is liable to little variation. If a day's labour of a working jeweller be more valuable than a day's labour of a common labourer, it has long ago been adjusted, and placed in its proper position in the scale of value."

And fifty years ago, when manufactures grew but slowly, and when the arts were comparatively stationary, this mode of speaking may not have been wholly incorrect—at any rate was not perfectly false. But now-a-days the different skill used in different employments varies incessantly; it tends to increase with every improvement in quality; it tends to diminish with every improvement in machinery. Even between the same employment at different times it is difficult to compare it, and between two different employments it is impossible to compare it. In a long time the circulation of labour from employment to employment no doubt brings about a rough and approximate equality. But this is only in a long time; it is a gradual and most incalculable operation. The cost of production would hardly, in any practical sense, determine price at all, if it only determined value after so many years and so irregularly. In fact, capital travels far quicker than labour, and there is some approximate equality between the products of two equal and similarly circumstanced capitals; and " cost of production," when analysed properly, is a prompt and effective regulator of " value".

But though Ricardo did not see this, as it is easy to see it now, he saw more clearly than many people now do that a rise of wages does not entail a rise of prices. As yet I can only deal with the case of a money-mining country ; a country of gold and silver mines; whether the fact that money—that the precious metals—are obtained by foreign trade, does, or does not, make a difference, will appear afterwards. But in the money-mining country nothing can be clearer. Nothing can change relative value except that which alters relative cost of production; what acts equally on all commodities will alter the exchangeable quality of none. If all equal capitals were spent in wages equally—say, if one-half of every £100 was always so spent in every trade, including money-mining—a rise, say, of twenty per cent. would not affect values at all. It would tell on gold-mining as well as on every other kind of production. "Hats," to take Ricardo's favourite article, would be produced at twenty per cent. more cost, but then sovereigns would be produced at twenty per cent. more cost also. And, therefore, there would be no more reason for raising the value of hats as against sovereigns than the value of sovereigns as against hats. The cause on one side is equal to the cause on the other.

This is at present curiously neglected in our common discussions. So far from Political Economy having advanced on this point since Ricardo's time, it—at least, the common exposition of it—has retrograded. In the incessant discussions of late years as to the effect of Trades Unions, it is perpetually assumed that, if these Unions extended to all employments, and if they produced a rise of wages in them all, they would certainly and necessarily produce a universal rise of prices. But the slightest thought would have shown that this rise, at least in a gold-mining country, would act on the gold as well as on the commodities exchanged for gold, and that the effect upon the one would counterbalance the effect upon the other.

Ricardo's conception of the cost of production was over-simplified; it left out part of the truth, and, consequently, gave an undue prominence to the other parts. But the slightest comparison between it and the ideas of Adam Smith will show how great is the advance which Political Economy has made between the two writers. Ricardo's is a first approximation to an exact science; Adam Smith's is but a set of popular conceptions—always sensible, but often discordant.

IV.

But it will be asked, if in each trading country the trader must receive the rate of profit of the country, —what is it which determines that rate of profit? And this is rather a long topic of inquiry.

For popular purposes, it is easy to say that the profit of a capitalist in any undertaking is that which remains after the cost of that undertaking has been satisfied. The outlay must be repaid, and what remains over is profit. But in an ordinary undertaking, say, in making cotton twist, there is this difficulty: a great deal of the outlay is upon machines and raw material, which are the results of previous undertakings, and which must in the long run be valued at the outlay on these undertakings, *plus* the profit at the rate of the time and country, and this profit is exactly what we are in search of. The common trade facts do not give us that which we want to know in a sufficiently simple form.

Supposing one capitalist ordered the whole article from the beginning; suppose the country was one in which cotton was grown; and suppose that the capitalist who grew it made all the necessary machines (including any preliminary ones necessary to make them), it is evident that his outlay would be of one sort, *wages* only. He would have to deal exclusively with labourers, for he would go himself to the root of the matter, and would employ the results of no previous capitals. His outlay would then consist of wages only, and his profit would be the amount remaining to him when that outlay was recouped. He would sell his article, and his profit would be the price, *minus* the wages paid.

This analogy represents the real facts much more accurately than would at first sight appear. Supposing the profits of all trades to be equal, it would represent them exactly. The manufacture of a consumable article is divided, say, into a hundred undertakings by various capitalists. If any one of these were—all things considered—more profitable than the others, capital would leave those others, and would collect in it. The natural tide of capital from the less to the more remunerative enterprise makes the profits in each part of an entire manufacture equal—which is as much as to say that it makes the entire manufacture just what it would have been had one single capitalist ordered or managed the whole of it from the very beginning to the very end. As we have seen, this doctrine of the equality of profit is but an approximation, but we have also seen that it is a most useful approximation, and what are the corrections to be made in using it. Subject to these corrections, therefore, we can say that the profit on an article—entirely made and manufactured in the same country—is the price of the article *minus* the wages spent on it. But we must reserve an inquiry into the possible profit where foreign materials and machines are used, for there is no transfer hither and thither of capitals between nations, and no consequent equality in the returns on them. We can only return to that case after examining the primitive simple one, where everything is made in the same country.

You say, I shall be told, that the profit is the selling price, *minus* the outlay, but you do not tell us what is the selling price. Nor can it be told without seeing how money is obtained. The price of a thing is the money for which it exchanges, and you must consider the nature of it before you can know what that price will be.

The money of commerce is composed of the precious metals—gold and silver—say, for shortness, gold, which is a commodity like any other. It is raised in the same way as iron, and according to the same laws. The capitalist must have in it the same profit that he has in other trades and no more. But the difference between it and other trades is that there is no need to sell the article. A capitalist raises so much gold, after a certain outlay; he can take that gold to the Mint, and the difference between it and the outlay is the profit. There is no haze about it; no difficult words such as price and value. It is a definite physical quantity—10,000 sovereigns were expended on the mine, and 11,000 came out, making a profit of 10 per cent. The standard rate of profit in money-mining is the rate of profit in the least productive money mine that can keep itself at work. All other profits compare themselves with that, for money is the standard of comparison, the reckoning engine.

Suppose it takes a third less labour and a third less machines to produce an ounce of gold; an ounce of gold will exchange for one-third less of other things; its buying power will be that much less; corn, cotton, and all other things, will exchange for so much more of it.

The money price of mining machinery will rise, the outlay of money necessary to work mines will augment, and the return to it, though greater in quantity, will be identical in proportion—will be the same rate per cent. The gold-mines which cannot pay that profit will be disused, just as old worn-out iron-mines are disused, and from the same cause—it no longer pays to work them. There will, however, be this difference, though the rate of profit in the gold trade will be the same, in other respects the trade will have changed. General prices will have altered.

In consequence, more money will be necessary to circulate the same commodities,—to do the same business. The same moneyed capital in the gold trade will produce the same number of sovereigns as before; it will yield as much per cent. The change will be, that the same " moneyed capital " will buy less labour and fewer machines, and the number of sovereigns that make the profit, though the same, will buy less of other things.

At every particular value of a sovereign there are a certain number of sovereigns required to carry on the business of a country. If more than that number is supplied, their value—their buying power—will diminish, and the price of all other things measured against them will rise. The machinery and labour by which sovereigns are made are a part of those other things, and their price will rise too. The outlay on the production of sovereigns will augment, and there will be a discouragement to produce them. The price in "sovereigns" of all other articles will have risen, as well as the outlay on their production; the apparent profit in producing them will, therefore, be as before. But though the outlay on a given number of sovereigns has risen, they are in no way better than before. There will, therefore, be a diminution in the production of sovereigns, and the number in circulation will be reduced to that required at cost value to conduct the trade of the country.

. . . .

The money rate of wages is a case of "supply and demand," using those words in the sense in which they have been explained—that is, it is determined by the amount of money which the owners of it wish to expend in labour, by the eagerness with which they want that labour, by the amount of labour in the market which wishes to sell itself for money, and by the eagerness with which the labourers desire that money. This, as we have seen, is peculiarly a case in which the market feelings of the two bodies of exchangers are carefully to be considered. If the labourers are in want, they must take whatever the capitalists offer them; if the capitalists are in want, they must buy the labour on the cheapest terms they can, but get it they must. And the capitalist is as likely, perhaps, to be in want as the labourer. It is true that the distress of the labourer is much more conspicuous, and that he advertises it; he goes about saying: "I am starving, and it is the tyranny of capital which is killing me". But it is also true that the capitalist is in danger of ruin, and that he conceals it. If he cannot complete contracts which he has made, if he has to stay out of a return from his business longer than he can afford, he is ruined. But he will never say this, because it may injure his credit and quicken the coming of the evil. He will lie awake with anxiety till his hair turns prematurely grey, and till deep lines of care form on his brow, but will say nothing. And it is necessary to insist on this now, because our current literature—some even of our gravest economic literature—is dangerously tainted with superficial sentiment. It speaks much of the sufferings of the working men which are seen, and little of those of the capitalist which are not seen. But the capitalist, being a higher and more thinking kind of man, is probably of more sensitive organisation than the labourer, and pecuniary anxiety is a more racking thing than any physical kind of pain short of extreme hunger. The mental feelings of the capitalist must just as much be regarded as those of the labourer in computing the rate at which the money of the one will be exchanged for the labour by the other.

The real remuneration of the labourer is, of course, not settled by this bargain. Money is of no use to him any more than to others, except for what it will fetch (indeed, as his wants are more immediate he feels this truth more than most others), and of what use it will be is settled by its purchasing power. This is again but a new case of supply and demand in the full sense of those terms. If the labourer is needy and has nothing beforehand, he will not be able to make his money go so far; he will be obliged to take anything which the shop-keeper will give him. At other times, he, like other people, may buy the goods of a bankrupt, "going at a sacrifice". He is also at the mercy of the other causes which raise the price of the articles on which he spends his money. A short harvest will send up the price excessively by diminishing the supply of food which the labourer wants more than anything else in the world; the passage of an army through the district will just as much effect this by introducing new mouths to be fed, who take the food with paying for it or without. The real remuneration of the labourer in commodities is settled by one case of ordinary exchange against money, just as the money price of that labour is settled by another.

It has, indeed, been contended that there is some-thing special in the article "labour" which affects this matter. It is said that if "labour" is not sold on a certain day—that is, if the labourer is idle—that labour is lost in consequence, whereas "com-modities" are permanent, and can be sold one day as well as another. But many commodities are, as we all know, very perishable, and are so without changing the principle on which their price is settled. And hiring a man and hiring a horse are obviously acts of the same species. The laws which settle monetary value are the same in the case of labour as in other cases.

·   ·   ·   ·   ·   ·   ·   ·   ·

APPENDIX.

NOTE A—(TO PAGE 139, LINE 16, AND TO PAGE 231, LINE 5).

The account of the market price given in the text, though long, and though, I trust, complete enough for its purpose, is not complete, and I should like to add to it a little. Political Economy tends to become unreal if it stands aloof from even the *minutiæ* of trading transactions.

First,—It is assumed in the text that the person who proposes to sell an article is possessed of it, is a "holder," as we say in market language; but nothing can be more untrue than to imagine that this is always so in markets. Many persons perpetually sell what they do not possess, and this great change, as is natural, makes other changes. The buyer's position is not, indeed, altered; very probably he neither cares nor knows whether the person proposing to deal with him does, or does not, possess the article; he thinks only whether the dealer will, or will not, be able to deliver it; if he gets it in time to satisfy the contract that is all which he cares for. But the seller has a new point to think of; not holding the article himself he must consider at what price he will be able to obtain it. This is by no means in all cases an easy matter. The Americans have invented a cant word for an organised mode of obstructing it. A "corner," in their language, is a gang of persons who, having heard that some one has need of a particular article, obtain possession of the whole supply of it in the market, and will only sell it to him at an excessive price. With the great articles of consumption this attempt is futile, the supply of them is too large, and too much divided; but with articles held by few dealers in small quantities— like many securities of minor importance on the Stock Exchange—such a plan is always possible and often profitable; and a person who sells what he has not got must reckon on the risk of it. This is one considerable change from the circumstances of ordinary bargains, and another is that no one makes a sale of this sort to obtain the means of meeting a liability.   In common business it often happens that a man must sell at a loss, because he has an " acceptance " to pay next day, and no other means of paying it.   But selling that which you do not possess, and which you must at once buy and pay for elsewhere, is of little use in such a strait.   It may bring a percentage of profit, but the *corpus* of the capital will not be available for the discharge of pre-existing liabilities ; it will be immediately paid out as part of the transaction which brought it in.

In this case, therefore, the first condition of the formula must be modified, and the early part of it will run : —

" A bargain will be struck when the seller thinks he cannot obtain more from the buyer with whom he is dealing, or from any other ;

" When he thinks he can himself obtain the article at a less price, and is willing to take the trouble and incur the risk of attempting to do so."

And the rest will stand as in the text.

Secondly,—There is a corresponding case in which the buyer has not the money, at least not nearly the whole of it, at the time he makes the bargain.   In Stock Exchange trans-actions this is exceedingly common.   Many buyers cannot pay for the securities they purchase except by ·mortgaging those securities ; many banks lend on them, taking a ten or a twenty per cent. margin, as it may be.   In the cotton and other produce markets there are similar loans.   The buyer has only a fraction of the purchase-money himself, he borrows the rest on the goods which are the subject matter of the transaction in order to complete it.   In this case, naturally, there are the two contrary peculiarities to the last ; the buyer has to consider whether he thinks he will be able to borrow the money, and whether the terms on which he will borrow it are good enough to make the transaction worth his while. There is, in this case, no fear of his being " cornered," at least not in a large money market like the English ; the voluntary operations of no gang, however powerful, would ever prevent the holder of good securities from obtaining money. But the involuntary circumstances of all dealers may prevent him. In a panic there may be no money to be obtained, and he may be ruined by being unable to complete his contract. And at a less excited moment scarcity of money may easily raise the rate of interest to a point so high as to turn the profit he expects on the transaction into a loss. In consequence, the second half of the first condition must be changed into this : —

"When the buyer thinks he can borrow the requisite money, and when he is sufficiently desirous of the article to make him take the trouble and incur the risk of attempting to do so ".

Till now, we have been speaking only of what are called "legitimate" transactions—bargains, that is, which are intended to be performed, and which mostly are performed. But there is another great class of contracts which are not intended to be performed according to their terms, and which are not so performed. These are "time bargains," of which there are some in most markets, but of which the Stock Exchange is the great seat. It is as common as anything here that a man should buy £20,000, say, " Peruvians," for a few days only, never intending to pay for them, and never intending to take them. The seller on his side understands that they are not meant either to be delivered, or to be paid for. The real contract is different from the verbal one; it is that on the day on which the bargain, according to its terms, is to be performed—the account day as it is called—the price of the bargain is to be compared with the price of the day, and that the buyer is to receive the difference, if the price of the day is the greater, and to pay the difference if the price of the bargain—the price at which he bought—is the greater. In plain English, if the price rises between the time of the purchase and the "settlement" the buyer is to have the difference; if it falls, the seller is to have it. The bargain is, in fact, a bet disguised as a sale. Each party is to win if the event he "backs" happens, and to lose if it does not. In this case the bargain will be struck :—

" When the buyer thinks he cannot induce the seller to fix a less price ;

"When he thinks this price likely to be less than the price on the future day of settlement ;

"When he thinks the chance of the difference he will receive, if his anticipation is right, worth the risk of that which he must pay, if his anticipation is wrong ;

"When the seller cannot induce the buyer to name a greater price, and when he thinks just the contrary as to these comparative prices and their resulting difference."

The "bulls" are speculators of this kind, who buy; and the "bears" speculators, who sell ; but the object of both is to gain the "difference": the former being sanguine, and thinking the price will rise; and the latter being gloomy, and expecting it to fall. It curiously happens, I believe, that the common outside public are almost always "bulls"—that is, take a cheerful view; and that it is the inside, or professional operator, who expects things to go down. And, of course, the sanguine people are those who lose ; the cool inside speculator lives on the folly of the outside world.

Time bargains are, more than any others, influenced by preceding bargains. When a stock is rising, many people will rush to bet that it will rise more ; when it is sinking, not so many people—but still many people—will be eager to bet that it will fall further. People who wish to bet on one side or the other naturally choose the side which is at the moment winning, unless they have a reason to the contrary—and many of these speculators seldom have much reason. In consequence, attempts to rig the market are more successful in this kind of business than in any other. A league of knowing speculators, which can make the market rise a little, will be sure to be imitated by a crowd of unknowing ones, and will be able to make money at their cost.

Of course it is possible to pursue these transactions upon a sound calculation. If a man has a real reason for thinking that a stock will ultimately rise very much, he may succeed by "time bargains" in it. But those who have a sound reason for what they do, and those who gain by it, are few in comparison with those who have only fancies, and who lose.

There is, too. an obvious defect in the formula of the text.

It treats "money," meaning all kinds of purchasing power, as if they were the same. But in reality they are different. "Cash" on delivery is better than a sale on credit, or than the best bill at a long rate. The ready-money price of a thing is, in consequence, always lower than the credit price;—at least it is so when the delivery of the article is equally immediate in the two cases. On the Stock Exchange, in the "Consol" market, for example, it is occasionally said that the "ready-money" price is greater than the price for the "account" (the account days are twice a month); but this only means that the stock is very scarce, and that in consequence it is much more convenient to deliver it a few days later than at once. The payment and the delivery are in both cases identical. Wherever there is a real sale on credit the price is always higher than in a sale for cash, because the buyer loses the use of the money for a time; and the credit price is sometimes much greater because the buyer may not be a man in much repute; and therefore, the seller may be disposed to ask a high premium for placing confidence in him, and he may be obliged to pay it.

The use of the formula given in the text will, however, lead to no mistake on this ground, when we know how to construe it. A credit price can at once be reduced to a cash price as soon as we know the time for which it was given, and the degree of trust reposed.

There are also two speculative difficulties which should be cleared away. It is often said that we ought to include in the term "supply," or whatever equivalent word we use, not merely the supply which is really in the market, but that which is coming to it—as it is phrased, the "prospective" supply, as well as the "actual". But I think that this would be a mistake. In the first place, it would be quite contrary to the ordinary phraseology of the markets; their language always distinguishes that which is on the spot as the supply *par excellence.* And it is always most unfortunate in an abstract theory to use a word in one sense which those who are most concerned with, and most practically skilled in, the subject of that theory use in a different sense. The consequent puzzles are incessant and important. And in this case the language of the market defines a vital distinction. There is a great difference between that part of the supply of a commodity which can, if its owners choose, be used to make good a contract, and that part which from distance or incompleteness of growth or make, cannot in physical possibility be so used. The actual supply for the purpose of any bargain is that with which the bargain can be performed; this is what ordinary dealers would say they dealt in. The coming supply, near or distant, certain or uncertain, complete or incomplete, influences the opinions of dealers and their wishes; it makes them more or less anxious to keep or to sell the actual supply but both in practical effect and in scientific conception the two are distinct.

It is also asked whether, when we say that " supply " influences price, we mean estimated supply or real supply. In the formula of the text, I have not used the word supply for fear of ambiguity, but have been careful to say " that I speak of the actual quantity" of the article in the market. The effect of this is very great, independently of the estimate of it, because the dealers who hold it, especially those who hold most of it, are in general somewhat anxious to be rid of it. What each man holds, and what he has to sell, is a much more vital thing to him than that which others hold; a little addition to his own stock is apt to influence him much more than a great increase to the stock in the hands of others. It is the "actual supply " which is the first force in the market, because each bit of it acts on the holder of that bit, and mostly guides him more than anything else.

Of course, however, the " estimated " supply—the notion every dealer has about the amount held by every other dealer—also influences all transactions. It acts on the mental element, —on opinion and on desire. According as it is less or more, it makes the seller less or more likely to think the article is likely to fall, and less or more anxious to dispose of it. But the estimate of one man will differ from that of another, and the effect on one will be counteracted by the effect on the other, —and we must not confound the chance results of these varying

opinions with the steady desire of each dealer to dispose of
his own article. In the language of the market, "supply"
means real supply, and in discussions about markets, it is
much the best to speak in the same way.

NOTE B—(TO PAGE 208).

After quoting Mr. Grote's judgment that Mill was unrivalled
in the power to compare opposite theories of the same
general facts, Mr. Bagehot, in the article we are quoting
from, which appeared in the *Economist* newspaper on the
17th May, 1873, thus proceeds: "In Political Economy
there was an eminent field for John Stuart Mill's peculiar
powers of comparison. There is little which is absolutely
original in his great work; and much of that little is not, we
think, of the highest value. The subject had been discussed
in detail by several minds of great acuteness and originality,
but no writer before Mill had ever surveyed it as a whole with
anything like equal ability; no one had shown with the same
fulness the relation which the different parts of the science
bore to each other; still less had any one so well explained
the relation of this science to other sciences, and to knowledge
in general. Since Mill wrote, there is no excuse for a Political
Economist if his teaching is narrow-minded or pedantic;
though, perhaps, from the isolated state of the science, there
may have been some before. Mill had another power, which
was almost of as much use to him for his special occupations,
as his power of writing, he was a most acute and discerning
reader. The world hardly gave him credit for this gift before
the publication of his book on Sir William Hamilton. But
those who have read that book will understand what Mr.
Grote means when, in his essay on Mill in the *Westminster
Review*, he speaks of Mill's 'unrivalled microscope which
detects the minutest breach or incoherence in the tissue of his
philosophical reasoning'. And Mill used this great faculty
both good-naturedly and conscientiously — he never gave
heedless pain to any writer, and never distorted any one's
meaning.

"In Political Economy the writer of these lines has long been in the habit of calling himself the last man of the ante-Mill period. He was just old enough to have acquired a certain knowledge of Ricardo and the other principal writers on Political Economy, before Mill's work was published; and the effect of it has certainly been most remarkable. All students since, begin with Mill and go back to all previous writers fresh from the study of him. They see the whole subject with Mill's eyes. They see in Ricardo and Adam Smith what he told them to see, and it is not easy to induce them to see anything else. Whether it has been altogether good for Political Economy that a single writer should have so monarchical an influence, may be argued, but no testimony can be greater to the ability of that writer and his pre-eminence over his contemporaries."

THE END.